SPEAKING ILL OF THE DEAD:

Jerks in Ohio History

SPEAKING ILL OF THE DEAD:
Jerks in Ohio History

Susan Sawyer

Globe
Pequot

Guilford, Connecticut

Globe Pequot

An imprint of Rowman & Littlefield

Distributed by NATIONAL BOOK NETWORK

British Library Cataloguing in Publication Information Available

Library of Congress Cataloging-in-Publication Data

Names: Sawyer, Susan, author.
Title: Speaking ill of the dead : jerks in Ohio history / Susan Sawyer.
Other titles: Jerks in Ohio history
Description: Guilford, Connecticut : Globe Pequot Press, 2016. | Series:
  Speaking ill of the dead | Includes bibliographical references and index.
Identifiers: LCCN 2016009249 (print) | LCCN 2016010784 (ebook) | ISBN
  9780762779161 (pbk.) | ISBN 9781493018925 (ebook)
Subjects: LCSH: Ohio—History—Anecdotes. | Ohio—Biography—Anecdotes. | Outlaws—
  Ohio—Biography—Anecdotes. | Rogues and vagabonds—Ohio—Biography—Anecdotes. |
  Criminals—Illinois—Ohio—Biography—Anecdotes.
Classification: LCC F491.6 .S29 2016 (print) | LCC F491.6 (ebook) | DDC
  364.3092/2771—dc23

Contents

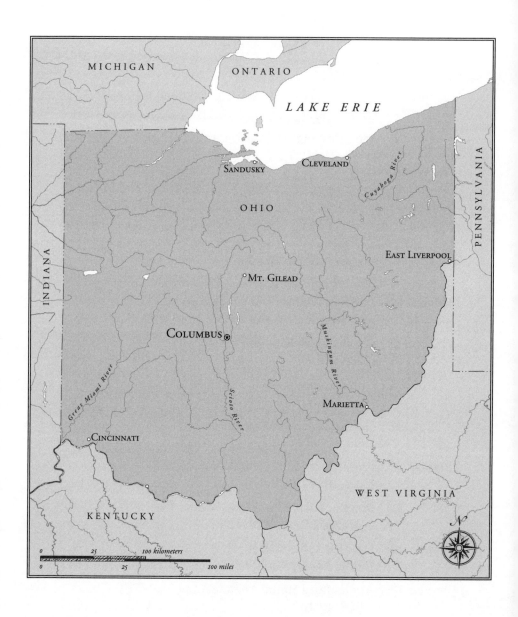

MICHIGAN

ONTARIO

LAKE ERIE

Sandusky

Cleveland

Cuyahoga River

OHIO

INDIANA

Mt. Gilead

East Liverpool

PENNSYLVANIA

Columbus

Muskingum River

Great Miami River

Scioto River

Marietta

Cincinnati

WEST VIRGINIA

KENTUCKY

0   25   100 kilometers

0   25   100 miles

N

CONTENTS

Dr. John Cook Bennett

The Diploma Peddler
1804-1867

In 1820 only two medical colleges had been established west of the Allegheny Mountains, and doctors were in short supply for the growing population. But a practicing Ohio physician found a way to confer medical degrees on anyone who wanted to become a doctor—and his unethical, illegal actions earned him the title of "The Diploma Peddler."

Dr. John Cook Bennett believed that medical degrees should be awarded on merit and not on the length of time spent in preparatory studies. Following the path of many aspiring physicians during the early decades of the nineteenth century, he obtained practical experience from a competent mentor. He then passed a lengthy examination issued by the state of Ohio and received a license to practice medicine. And in spite of his beliefs that a medical education was not necessary to become proficient in medicine, he made numerous attempts to establish several medical colleges— and funded his endeavors by selling bogus medical diplomas.

Born in Fairhaven, Massachusetts, on August 3, 1804, John Cook Bennett was the oldest child of Abigail Cook and John Bennett. At a young age he and his family moved to Marietta, Ohio, to join other family members who had already settled there. Few facts are available about his childhood, other than he was raised in southeastern Ohio. Although Bennett claimed to be a graduate of Ohio University, records of his attendance or graduation have never been found.

Since a lack of finances prohibited Bennett from attending one of the two medical colleges in the region—Transylvania

University in Lexington, Kentucky, and the Ohio Medical College in Cincinnati—he turned to his uncle, Dr. Samuel P. Hildreth, for guidance. A respected physician in the region, Hildreth took his eighteen-year-old nephew under his wing for a medical preceptorship in 1822.

Bennett was a diligent medical apprentice under Hildreth, traveling with his uncle throughout southeastern Ohio and portions of neighboring states, treating patients, and gaining practical experience along the way. He also studied standard medical texts, along with Latin and Greek, to prepare for the state medical exam. On November 1, 1825, he traveled to Meigs County, Ohio, to take his medical examination. He passed the exam with ease and officially became a licensed physician.

By passing the medical exam, Bennett legally earned the right to practice medicine. But successfully demonstrating his proficiency on the test did not give him the privilege of using the term "MD" after his name. Medical degrees were hard to attain at the time, and many competent physicians did not have a degree from a medical college. Still, holding an MD signified that the possessor was a medical authority, and the public appreciated the status of physicians who had obtained medical degrees.

In January 1826 Bennett married Mary Barker in Wisemans Bottom, a small community near Marietta. For the next four years, the young couple moved from place to place in Ohio. They established their first home in St. Clairsville, the Belmont County seat. Bennett quickly became active in the community, joining the medical society and the Masons. The following year the Bennetts moved to McConnelsville and welcomed their first child, Mary, into the world sometime during late 1827 or early 1828.

The Bennetts' next move was to Circleville, the seat of Pickaway County, in 1828. In this small town south of Columbus, Bennett opened a medical practice. By the end of the year, he claimed to be generating a lucrative income from his practice, averaging four to twelve dollars a day. Around the same time, the Bennetts welcomed the birth of their second child, Joseph, but the baby only lived for a few days. During their stay in Circleville, Bennett fought against a measles epidemic and was engaged in a variety of other activities.

In August 1829 the Bennetts relocated to Malta, on the west bank of the Muskingum opposite McConnelsville. A short time later they moved to Barnesville, a small town eighteen miles from their first home in St. Clairsville.

In Barnesville Bennett set up his medical practice in partnership with Dr. John Gladstone Affleck, who had been educated in Glasgow, Scotland. Some historians contend that Affleck encouraged Bennett to take medical courses at McGill College in Montreal. Bennett later claimed he attended lectures in Montreal and received a medical degree from the College Medical d'Emulation, although no records have been found to document his statement or verify the existence of the medical college. Nonetheless, by July 1831 Bennett was claiming to hold a medical degree, adding "MD" after his name.

During his early years as a physician in Ohio, Bennett advertised his services in newspapers, establishing visibility throughout the state as a notable physician. Even though he had never attended medical school, he also established legitimacy for himself by writing and submitting articles to professional medical journals.

Outside of medicine Bennett served as a traveling minister, preaching in several Methodist Episcopal churches in Ohio. He occasionally signed his name as the "Rev. Doctor John Cook Bennett." Raised as a Methodist and married in the Methodist church, Bennett abruptly switched to the primitive Christian church around 1830. The movement, advocated by Thomas Campbell and his son, Alexander, abandoned sectarian creeds and supported "primitive Christianity." The church was known by several names, including the Christian Disciples and the Disciples of Christ.

His sudden shift to the Christian church apparently stemmed from ulterior motives. For some time Bennett had wanted to establish a university in Ohio. Since the formation of a college required approval by the state legislature, Bennett launched a drive to gain support for a college from members of the Ohio legislature. With few personal finances to back the venture, he also pleaded for financial support from the Ohio Annual Conference of the Methodist Associate Church in 1831. When the church delayed consideration of his request to the next annual meeting, Bennett suspected the group was stalling on his request and promptly left the Methodist denomination. He immediately switched his allegiances to the Christian Disciples in hopes of gaining their financial support to launch the college.

With the support of Alexander Campbell, Bennett attempted unsuccessfully to launch colleges in Ohio and Virginia. By late 1832, however, Bennett's luck changed. The citizens of New Albany, Indiana, welcomed the idea of a college in their town. The *New Albany Gazette* even predicted the town would "reap great advantages from it."

In December 1832 a Floyd County representative petitioned the Indiana General Assembly to incorporate a Christian College in New Albany. John Cook Bennett was named in the petition as the college's agent, president, and bishop. The house and the senate approved the bill in early 1833. Bennett immediately arrived in New Albany and started advertising his medical services.

The first meeting of Christian College trustees took place in Bennett's home. Instead of serving as president, as stated in the petition, Bennett was elected to the position of chancellor. In this role he had the authority to preside at trustees' meetings, confer degrees, and remove officers or faculty members. Prominent leaders of the Christian church from Virginia, Ohio, Kentucky, and Indiana were elected officers, and faculty members were appointed.

The group also adopted several innovative bylaws, including offering doctorates in fifteen academic subjects. At the time, colleges and universities only offered doctorate degrees in medicine, theology, and law. Bennett strongly advocated allowing women to pursue medical degrees at Christian College, but other trustees staunchly opposed the proposal. He finally agreed to prohibit females from receiving medical degrees, and the group agreed that women could still earn doctorates in seven other areas of study. As a result Christian College became one of the first publicly chartered coeducational colleges in America.

Another provision allowed Christian College to award diplomas based upon successful passage of a medical exam without regard to "the length of time spent in preparatory studies."

The bylaws also stated that "persons self-taught or taught anywhere in public or private schools . . . who shall stand an examination in any department for which degrees shall be conferred, shall obtain such degrees as they are entitled to from merit."

Bennett believed that the medical schools' requirement for a specified term of study was based upon "purely mercenary considerations." He pointed out that other colleges had similar provisions. The University of Virginia, for instance, permitted the granting of medical degrees without reference to the time spent studying medicine as long as candidates passed appropriate examinations. In fact, until after the Civil War many colleges granted various degrees based upon examination alone.

With officers elected, faculty members appointed, and bylaws approved, Christian College appeared to be ready to open its doors. But Bennett had failed to get advance approval from numerous individuals as to their willingness to serve as college officers and faculty members. He may have assumed that leaders of the Christian church and fellow physicians would be more than happy to support the endeavor, or he may have been so anxious to launch the college that he leaped ahead and named the officers and staff without consulting anyone. Most likely, however, he may have been setting the stage for other fraudulent activities in his future.

No matter his motivations, Bennett's actions created an uproar among his colleagues. One leader in the Christian church, Barton W. Stone, discovered he had been elected to serve as a vice president of the college when he read the news in the *New Albany Gazette*. Stone also contended he "had no knowledge, nor hint that application was to be made to the legislature for such a charter, or had been made, or granted." He also claimed he was ignorant "of the appointment of presidents, vice presidents, secretaries and all other officers, till informed by the same journal."

Walter Scott, another church leader, claimed that he had first heard about the college when he received a letter stating he had been unanimously elected "President of the Faculty." Scott viewed this "as an absolute forgery" and "declined every and all connection" with the school.

Alexander Campbell, the head of the Christian church, was also dismayed by Bennett's underhanded ways, stating that it would "have been more respectful to the judgment and wishes of the brethren to have consulted them on the propriety of such a scheme." He also claimed to be stunned that Bennett had pressed forward with establishing a Christian college in Indiana. After Bennett's unsuccessful attempts to charter other colleges in Ohio and Virginia, Campbell had assumed that Bennett "had given it up." Now, with Bennett's lack of consideration for church leaders, Campbell wanted to end the connection between the college and the Christian church.

To appease Campbell, the trustees passed an ordinance at the second meeting of Christian College to change the name of the institution to the "University of Indiana, at New Albany." They would also retain the name of Christian College as required by their charter. Oddly enough, Campbell seemed pleased with this strategy, indicating that "as a literary institution, liberal and anti-sectarian, we wish it all success."

Lack of support from Campbell, Scott, Stone, and other Christian ministers meant that Bennett could not count on financial support or fund-raising activities within the Christian church—support that he desperately needed to launch the college. Before the Civil War, approximately four out of five new colleges never succeeded due to financial woes.

To generate revenue, Bennett came up with an ingenious, yet unscrupulous, idea. He decided to confer medical degrees on anyone who seemed qualified and provide a diploma as proof of the degree. Each recipient would pay ten dollars for the privilege of receiving the diploma. The fee was reasonable, he assessed, since medical colleges typically charged students much more. Moreover, the price would not only cover his expenses for printing the diplomas but also leave him with a tidy profit. To take full advantage of potential customers seeking diplomas, he also decided to confer advanced degrees for other academic areas such as law, theology, and the arts and sciences.

Bennett lithographed hundreds of diplomas that were engraved with the seal of the corporation of the Christian College. Bennett's signature, as well as the signatures of the dean and registrar of the college, were also lithographed. Blank areas were reserved to pen the name of the recipient and the date that the degree was conferred.

In May 1833 the *New Albany Gazette* reported that Bennett planned to travel east "to procure some Anatomical preparations for the College, and to make arrangements for the University in general." In reality Bennett was traveling throughout the midwestern and eastern states conferring MAs, DDs, LLDs, and MDs for ten dollars each.

Word soon spread of Bennett's fraudulent activities. Scott insisted the scoundrel "rained down his L.L.D.'s, D.D.'s, A.B's., & A.M.'s, like a shower of hail." Another critic reported that Bennett dispensed the "diplomas to every ignoramus who could raise ten dollars to buy one . . . though they were not worth a cent." And one man claimed that Bennett "lavished his diplomas upon various gentlemen of the different sects in different parts of the United States" and questioned "the purity of his motives."

In reality Bennett had few, if any, qualifications that justified his examining anyone or conferring degrees in these areas. At the time, MAs (or AMs) were mainly honorary degrees. In the 1830s no position in the United States required an MA degree.

Bennett apparently ignored his critics and expanded his dishonest activities by recruiting two New York physicians, both members of the New York County Medical Society, to examine prospective students and confer degrees in New York for the sum of twenty-five dollars. The Christian College bylaws, he insisted, authorized him to send out other commissioners to confer degrees.

Throughout the summer and fall of 1833, Bennett and his two New York colleagues conferred hundreds of degrees in the area. They allegedly granted diplomas to many student residents without examinations, and one recipient was not even in the city at the time the degree was conferred.

By the end of the year, the New York County Medical Society had caught onto Bennett's deceitful activities. On December 16, 1833, a committee appointed by the society reported they had made a "diligent search" into "the character and validity of Diplomas of the degree of Doctor of Medicine" issued by the "University of Indiana." The group also contended that the granting of diplomas was illegal in New York and proceeded to pass along their findings to the New York legislature and the governor of Indiana. James R. Manley, who would later become president of the New York County Medical Society, reported that Bennett sold the degrees "about the country at various prices, like the merchandize of an itinerant peddler."

Meanwhile, Bennett had returned to Ohio, opened an office in Columbus, and placed advertisements in the *Ohio State Journal* for his medical services. Moreover, he made plans to create another university, "The Classical, Literary, and Scientific Institution of the Scioto Valley," in Franklin County. After a brief period of lobbying state legislators, the bill passed the Ohio House of Representatives in December 1833, with little discussion.

Upon learning about Bennett's latest quest to establish another college, Dr. Thomas Morrow, president of a small sectarian college in Worthington, Ohio, quickly informed the chairman of the Ohio Senate Standing Committee on Colleges and Universities of Bennett's history of selling medical degrees. Morrow's Ohio Reformed Medical College was located only a few miles away from Bennett's proposed college, and Morrow adamantly opposed the creation of a nearby rival college by the unscrupulous Bennett.

An investigation by a senate committee discovered that most of the names included in Bennett's petition to establish the college had been used without prior knowledge or consent, and only four of the forty-nine petitioners were Ohio residents. When the committee reported that Bennett was "a notorious individual" with "sinister" motives in trying to create the university, the Ohio senate unanimously rejected the bill.

In spite of the New York and Ohio allegations against him, Bennett attempted to continue his duplicitous activities. He soon discovered, however, that word had spread about his history of selling fake diplomas. Early in 1834 Bennett applied to the Board of Trustees of the Granville Baptist College to help establish a medical department at the college. The trustees swiftly rejected his application, apparently aware of his dubious actions.

Undeterred by the rebuff, Bennett moved forward and contacted the trustees of Willoughby University of Lake Erie in Chagrin, Ohio, in July 1834. In a letter to the trustees, signed by "J. C. Bennett" from South Bloomfield, Ohio, Bennett offered to establish a medical college at the university. The group swiftly accepted the offer, and Bennett became an honorary trustee with an appointment as a professor of midwifery. Within a short time he was also elected by faculty members to serve as president of the medical college.

In spite of his position at Willoughby University, Bennett continued to sell diplomas during his travels. He insisted he had the right to confer degrees from Christian College for ten years, the period of time that prohibited the Indiana legislature from amending the college's charter. In October 1834, for instance, he visited both New York and Boston on the pretense of raising funds for Willoughby. In actuality he was selling degrees from Christian College.

By the end of the year, Bennett's charade abruptly ended. Publicly identified as the "Diploma Peddler," he was fired from Willoughby University at the end of the first term. Moreover, the Christian church denounced any further association with Bennett in 1835. Scott stated he was a vagabond without character, "a false brother and an imposter, a person of no solid learning and of very bad morals." Other leaders of the church disclaimed "all connection with Mr. Bennett."

Though Bennett claimed to be awarding degrees to raise funds for Christian College, he apparently pocketed the funds from the sale of diplomas. He never accounted for his expenses or the funds generated from selling degrees. In fact, two eyewitnesses claimed to have seen him gambling, and one source accused him of speculating in Michigan real estate.

Moreover, no records have been found of any meetings of the trustees of Christian College after April 1833. College courses were never offered at Christian College, and property and facilities were never acquired. Worse yet, Bennett was never held liable for his scams. Despite the actions of the New York County Medical Society and the Ohio legislature, neither the Indiana governor nor the state legislature examined Bennett's activities. The charter of Christian College was not repealed.

Since Bennett was never held accountable for his actions, he continued to engage in a number of questionable schemes and activities. In 1840 he moved to Nauvoo, Illinois, and joined the Mormon Church. He became an active leader in the community and successfully lobbied the Illinois legislature to pass an act for the incorporation of Nauvoo University. As president he conferred LLDs upon select prominent Americans such as James G. Bennett, editor of the *New York Herald*. During this time he also became a close friend of Joseph Smith, leader of the Mormon Church.

In February 1841 Bennett was elected as the first mayor of Nauvoo. Impressed with Bennett's accomplishments and influence among the townspeople, Smith appointed Bennett as assistant president of the church.

The following year a series of events revealed that Bennett's despicable lack of character had not changed. When Smith discovered that Bennett was leading a secret life of adultery, spreading lies about Smith and church doctrine, and planning a possible assassination attempt on Smith's life, Bennett was removed from his civil positions and excommunicated from the church.

Seeking revenge, Bennett published a book, *The History of the Saints: or an Exposé of Joe Smith and the Mormons*, with accusations against the church that ranged from murder to overthrowing the government. The Mormon Church considers Bennett to be the "most notorious" of the apostates of the church.

In the late 1840s Bennett moved to Massachusetts, where he focused his attention on raising poultry. He even sponsored a poultry convention in Boston in 1849 that attracted more than ten thousand participants. Five years later, he moved to Polk City, Iowa. He remained in Iowa until his death in 1867 at the age of sixty-three.

John Chivington

The Fighting Parson
1821–1894

John Chivington stepped up to the pulpit, Bible in hand, acutely aware that not everyone in his congregation at the Methodist church in Platte County, Missouri, agreed with his stance against slavery in 1856. In fact, pro-slavery church members had threatened to tar and feather him if he spoke out against slavery at the next Sunday service.

Undeterred by the threats, Chivington took his place behind the pulpit. Standing over six feet, four inches and weighing 260 pounds, he loomed over the congregation. After placing the Bible on the pulpit, he pulled out two pistols and placed the weapons beside the Bible. "By the grace of God and these two revolvers, I am going to preach here today."

With his statement and actions on that Sunday morning, Chivington soon became known as the "Fighting Parson." Less than ten years later, his fighting spirit would also lead to the massacre of a sleeping Indian village, an event that would label him the "butcher of Sand Creek."

Born on January 27, 1821, John Milton Chivington was the son of Isaac and Jane Runyon Chivington, who had settled in Warren County, Ohio, around 1810. The family made a home in the wilderness near Lebanon, about twenty miles northeast of Cincinnati. Isaac farmed and harvested timber from his vast acreage to support his growing family. All six of the Chivington children were born in the family's small cabin: Lewis, Sarah, John, Isaac, and two babies who died during infancy.

Isaac died in 1826, leaving Jane to support the family. Lewis, the oldest son, took over the timber business, while the younger children helped their mother cultivate the land for farming. Only five years old at the time of his father's death, young John Chivington learned to read from his mother with only the Bible and a few other books in the home.

At age thirteen Chivington went to work with his brother in the timber business. Five years later he assumed the duties of finding prospective buyers for the family's product and frequently traveled to Cincinnati to call on customers. Martha Rollason, a young woman in the city who worked for one of Chivington's friends, soon caught Chivington's eye. Romance quickly blossomed, and the couple wed in late 1840. To support his wife, Chivington became a carpenter's apprentice.

Chivington worked diligently at his trade while the young couple started their family. Their son, Thomas, was born in 1841. The Chivingtons also welcomed two daughters into the world: Elizabeth Jane, born in 1842, and Sarah, in 1844.

While attending a revival meeting in 1842, Chivington experienced a religious conversion and became a member of the Methodist church. Within a short time he felt called to enter the ministry and consulted with the Methodist bishop of southern Ohio. To prepare for the ministry, the bishop suggested he study the Bible and church doctrine and gain some preaching experience from the pulpit as a deacon.

During the following two years, Chivington worked at his trade during the day and studied for the ministry at night. By September 1844 he had finished his studies, become an ordained minister, and was assigned to the Zoar Church in the Goshen Circuit of the Ohio Conference.

Chivington willingly relocated his family from place to place over the next ten years, serving in parishes in Illinois, Missouri, and Kansas. He frequently traveled by horseback to small communities as a circuit rider, spreading the gospel along the way. He also worked as a missionary to the Wyandot Indians in Kansas for a time before serving as presiding elder at the Methodist Episcopal Church in St. Joseph, Missouri.

By the mid-1850s Chivington was voicing his stance against slavery from the pulpit at every opportunity. Though pro-slavery members of Chivington's congregation at the Methodist church in Platte County, Missouri, backed down from their threat to harm their minister, the Methodist church decided to remove Chivington from the dangerous atmosphere in the slave state of Missouri. The Chivingtons relocated to Omaha, Nebraska.

While in Nebraska Chivington earned a reputation as a "sound theologian" and "a man of extraordinary natural abilities, destined to make his mark in the religious world," reported the *Nebraska Advertiser* in Brownville. Moreover, the Methodist Episcopal Church appointed Chivington as presiding elder of the Omaha District in 1857, and he served the Nebraska City District in the same capacity for the following two years.

The Methodist Episcopal Church recognized Chivington's abilities and advanced him to serve as presiding elder of Colorado's Rocky Mountain District in 1860. But the outbreak of the Civil War convinced Chivington that he had to join the Union forces and fight against slavery. Though the governor of Colorado Territory offered to commission Chivington as a regimental chaplain, he refused the appointment and requested a commission as a soldier. In 1861 he was appointed as major of the First Colorado Regiment.

In February 1862 the regiment was ordered to ward off an attack by Confederates in New Mexico. A member of the regiment later recalled the image of Chivington in battle, stating that a Confederate officer "emptied his revolvers three times at the Major and then made his company fire a volley at him. As if possessed of a charmed life, he galloped unhurt through the storm of bullets."

Under Chivington's command his troops captured a Confederate supply train in a surprise attack and burned the entire train of crucial provisions. Proving to be a capable, competent soldier, Chivington was praised by his superiors for his actions. He was soon appointed to the rank of colonel.

Colonel John M. Chivington

Having tasted success as a soldier, Chivington aspired to higher positions of power. Hoping to obtain an appointment to the rank of brigadier general, he traveled to Washington with an endorsement from Colorado governor John Evans. Secretary of War Edwin Stanton, however, did not confirm the promotion.

In 1864 Chivington was appointed commander of the Military District of Colorado. At dawn on November 29, 1864, Chivington led an estimated seven hundred soldiers from the Third and First Colorado Cavalry regiments on a surprise attack on a Cheyenne village at Sand Creek. The troops charged into the village and killed at least 150 men, women, and children of the Cheyenne and Arapaho tribes.

Not satisfied with merely killing the residents of the village, the soldiers spent the afternoon of the attack and the following day scalping and mutilating the bodies. When the troops returned to Denver on December 22, they paraded through the streets, proudly flaunting their "trophies" from the attack.

Initially Chivington was hailed as a hero for the attack on the Cheyenne village. The *Rocky Mountain News* claimed the campaign was "brilliant," and the *Nebraska City News* insisted that "the people of Colorado, Idaho, Montana, and Nebraska will ever think he did right." By the end of the year, however, other newspapers were reporting that soldiers involved in the attack "do not scruple to say that the big battle of Sand Creek was a cold-blooded massacre." Word of the slaughter also reached Washington, and soon three separate federal investigations were launched.

Outside the western territories, newspapers took the opposite stance. An editorial in the *Chicago Tribune* on July 26, 1865, called the battle "an act of hideous cruelty, garnished with all the accessories of fraud, lying, treachery, and beastially [sic]" and recommended that "Colonel Chivington ought to be tried by a court-martial and shot like a wolf" for his actions at Sand Creek.

Although all three inquiries into the Sand Creek murders severely criticized his conduct, Chivington never faced a court-martial. Conveniently, his commission expired on January 4, 1865.

With his ministerial and military careers behind him, Chivington launched a campaign to run for Congress from Colorado in October 1865. His former troops campaigned on his behalf, and supporters greeted him warmly at a campaign appearance in Denver. But Chivington could not overcome the intense criticism of the Sand Creek massacre. Within a month after announcing his candidacy for Congress, he withdrew from the race.

Since Chivington no longer earned an income from the church or the military, he moved back to Nebraska in 1866 and joined his son, Thomas, and son-in-law, Thomas Pollack, in their successful freight business. Soon he was leading wagon trains, hauling freight from Nebraska to Kansas and other western locations.

Only months after Chivington joined the freight business, a series of cruel tragedies struck the Chivington family. In June 1866 his only son, Thomas, drowned while trying to retrieve a ferryboat that had broken loose from a landing on the North Platte River in present-day Wyoming. Thomas's grieving widow, Sarah, gave birth to the couple's third child, Thomas M. Chivington, only six weeks after the accident. Less than a year later, Lulu, the two-year-old daughter of Thomas and Sarah Chivington, also drowned when she fell overboard from a steamboat on the Missouri River. The *Nebraska Herald* reported, "Almost superhuman efforts were made by the Captain to recover her . . . but she was never seen again." The third blow to the family occurred shortly after Lulu's death when Chivington's wife, Martha, died in Cass County, Nebraska, at a Methodist camp meeting.

The events that unfolded after the three deaths shocked both the public and close friends of the Chivington family. In his role as administrator of his son's estate, Chivington pushed the boundaries of his obligations by filing claims on behalf of the estate for his own benefit. However, Chivington was not the heir to the estate. The rightful heir was Thomas's widow, Sarah.

Apparently motivated by greed to gain control of his son's estate, Chivington took the unprecedented move of proposing marriage to his former daughter-in-law, who was twenty years his junior. On May 13, 1868, forty-seven-year-old John Chivington married his son's widow in Chicago's Methodist Episcopal Church.

Sarah's parents were horrified and outraged. In a letter to the *Nebraska City News*, they claimed the marriage was a "Criminal act . . . unknown to us." If they had been aware of the exchange of vows, they insisted "some measures would have been taken to prevent the consummation of so vile an outrage—even if violent measures were necessary." Even the *New York Times* noted the unusual coupling, reporting the event with the headline, "A Strange Marriage."

John and Sarah Chivington immediately moved to Omaha to begin their married life. From the beginning Sarah was acutely aware of her new husband's greediness and unethical behavior. In later years she claimed Chivington was fired from his job at the Omaha office of the Washington Life Insurance Company of New York for doing "crooked work."

The following year they returned to Nebraska City and moved into the home that Sarah had once shared with her first husband. Within a short time a fire broke out in the house. Sarah suspected that Chivington had purposely set the fire to file an insurance claim on the property. But his devious plan to pocket $4,000 in cash from an insurance policy was unsuccessful. The flames destroyed only a few pieces of furniture worth $175.

With the meager proceeds from the insurance claim, the couple headed to Washington, DC. In the nation's capital Chivington proceeded to file yet another claim for losses incurred by his son. Insisting he was seeking compensation on behalf of his son's estate, Chivington sought payment for the loss of several horses that had been stolen by Indians while Thomas was hauling freight in 1864. He soon discovered that another freight hauler had already received a settlement in the case. The hauler, however, offered to split the settlement if Chivington provided an indemnifying bond.

Although Chivington provided a bond allegedly signed by Nebraska's US senator, Thomas W. Tipton, authorities discovered Tipton's signature was a forgery and the seal used to make the notary's mark on the document had been stolen. Federal authorities were notified, an indictment was sought, and Chivington was arrested.

The *Washington Star and Chronicle* not only reported Chivington's arrest, but also published an article about Chivington's later appearance in police court on the charge that he "grossly insulted a lady." It was alleged that he had knocked down a woman on the street in Washington.

Without a source of income, the Chivingtons traveled to New York and spent several months with members of Sarah's family. True to his character, Chivington borrowed money from family members and never bothered to repay the funds.

Chivington continued to evade any consequences for his actions, even though his behavior was less than honorable. In 1869 he appeared before the Nebraska Methodist Episcopal Conference on charges relating to his character. Church officials determined that the questions surrounding his behavior were not serious enough to dismiss him from the church.

In November 1870 Sarah traveled to Nebraska City to visit her parents while Chivington stayed in Washington, attempting to file more claims. Though she expected him to meet her in Nebraska after he settled his business matters, Chivington never arrived. "He left for parts unknown," Sarah later explained. After months passed with no word of her husband, Sarah filed for divorce on the grounds of nonsupport. The divorce was officially granted in 1871. In her later years Sarah voluntarily testified against Chivington when he filed claims for pension and Indian depredation, strongly believing he was undeserving of any compensation.

Years later Chivington admitted he never returned to Sarah, choosing instead to visit Canada for three weeks and then Mexico for the following two months. Eventually he returned to his native Ohio after receiving word that his mother was gravely ill. He later stated, "She lingered for seven years, and I felt it to be my duty to remain and sustain one to whom I owed so much in her declining years."

Still, Chivington continued his greedy ways. One gentleman reported that Chivington took eighty dollars that his mother had set aside for her burial expenses and spent the funds on a suit of clothing. The township ended up paying for his mother's burial expenses.

Chivington married a third time on November 25, 1873, to widow Isabella Amzen of Cincinnati. Though he fully intended to return to Denver with his new wife, Isabella had no desire to leave Ohio. When a fire destroyed the newlyweds' house on their farm in Warren County, the Chivingtons moved to Blanchester, in Clinton County. While residing in Blanchester, Chivington launched a new career as editor and publisher of a small newspaper, *The Press*.

But all was not blissful in the Chivington household. The third Mrs. Chivington soon pressed charges against her husband for theft and assault. Isabella, who appeared in court with a black eye and facial bruises, claimed he had not only stolen a promissory note that belonged to her, but also forged her name to the note, collected the money, and beat her when she questioned him about it.

Chivington was arrested and bound over to a Blanchester court on charges of assault. However, Isabella apparently had a change of heart and dropped the charges on the condition that Chivington would pay the court costs—which he never did. Nonetheless, Isabella remained married to John Chivington for the rest of his life.

Outside his personal life, Chivington could not resist the prospect of entering the political arena. In 1883 he announced his candidacy as the Republican delegate for the Ohio State Legislature. But local newspapers immediately reminded the public of his role in the Sand Creek massacre and recounted some sordid details about his personal life. "Hypocrisy and deceit are distinguishing characteristics of his being," stated an article in the *Clinton County Democrat*. "Under the cloak of religion he seeks to hide the deformity of his moral nature." Though Chivington believed a longtime rival was responsible for spreading malicious rumors about him, the negativity from the press forced his withdrawal from the race.

In the midst of the controversy, Chivington eagerly accepted an invitation to speak before the Pioneers of Colorado in Denver. In September 1883 he stood before the crowd and defiantly stated, "I stand by Sand Creek." He was so enthused by the welcoming reception in Denver that he and Isabella moved to the city.

While living in Denver, Chivington wrote a series of articles that recalled his early career in the First Colorado Volunteers. He was elected president of the Colorado veterans' association and stepped back into the pulpit at several Methodist churches. He also held a series of jobs, first as undersheriff of Arapahoe County and later as coroner.

But controversy erupted again. As the *Denver Republican* explained, Chivington had submitted a bill for twenty-five days of services as bailiff in the district court at $2.50 per day. He also had claimed expenses for traveling 522 miles during the month of May. Suspecting he had grossly exaggerated his claims, the county commissioners investigated the account. As undersheriff, he was charged with perjury.

After a short trial Chivington was acquitted, once again escaping punishment for his underhanded actions. The court ruled that he could not be punished for perjury because of the form of the oath that he took.

Still, Chivington's troubles continued. In 1892 he was accused of stealing money from a corpse while rendering services as a coroner. A petition filed in Arapahoe County on behalf of the estate of Francesco Gallo alleged he had stolen eight hundred dollars from Gallo. The court ordered Chivington to return the money, less any expenses for his services as coroner. Chivington did not deny he had taken the money, but he did not return the funds. Instead he submitted a bill to the estate for $182.

During his remaining years Chivington battled severe illnesses and continued to file claims against the federal government. In his quest to obtain a military pension in 1891, he claimed that during his service his horse had fallen on him, badly injuring his ankle, knee, and hip joints and leaving his left leg quite lame.

He also claimed to suffer from chronic dysentery. Not surprisingly, the government denied his claim.

He also filed a depredation claim against the Oglala Sioux in 1891, seeking nearly thirty-three thousand dollars in damages. The assistant attorney general filed a counter claim, asserting that the damages suffered by the Indians at Sand Creek were "an amount far exceeding in value that of the claimant's claim." Once again, Chivington's claim was denied by the federal government.

Chivington died on October 4, 1894, at age seventy-three. The funeral service, held at Denver's Trinity United Methodist Church, was conducted with full Masonic honors. Ignoring the misdeeds of Chivington's life, the minister praised Chivington during the eulogy. "He towered above other men like a California redwood tree above the other trees of the forest, and I could never see him without envying his superb physique," the minister declared. "We shall not look upon his like again."

Chivington was buried in Denver's Fairmount Cemetery. No doubt the Ohio native made his mark as a charismatic military leader and powerful Methodist minister. But the life of John Milton Chivington is primarily remembered for the Sand Creek massacre of innocent Indians and his personal flaws of greed, dishonesty, and total lack of integrity.

George H. Devol

King of the Riverboat Gamblers
1829–1903

The pungent aroma of cigars wafted through the saloon on the *Eclipse* during its maiden voyage on the mighty Mississippi River. As the steamer chugged its way to New Orleans, a large, muscular man sat at one of the tables in the steamer's bar and studied the cards in his hand. The man was George Howard Devol, known as the "King of the Riverboat Gamblers" during the heyday of riverboat travel during the mid-nineteenth century. The two men playing poker with him, however, had no idea of the man's true identity. They took the man at his word when he proclaimed his occupation was a "horseman."

The three men played several hands of poker. George, eager to gain the men's confidence that he was a mere traveler who played an honest game, maintained a mild, easygoing temperament as he dealt each hand. After several games the two men retired to their cabins for the evening. George went to his cabin as well, but soon returned to the bar. He handed over six decks of marked cards to the barkeeper, requesting the cards be sent to the table where he would be playing poker the next morning.

At first the barkeeper refused George's request, fearing he might lose his job if he were caught. But George convinced him that the deception would be perfectly safe. These were his personal marks on the cards that might only be detectable to older, more seasoned gamblers, he insisted.

The barkeeper relented to George's wish. When the gambler returned to the bar the next morning, he was pleased to see his cards on the table. Soon the two travelers joined George, the cards

George H. Devol
COURTESY, LIBRARY OF CONGRESS

were dealt, and the games began. By the time the *Eclipse* arrived in New Orleans that evening, George had won more than four thousand dollars. The two men left the steamer, unaware their pockets had been emptied by the master of the riverboat gamblers. And they had no idea that George had handed over a generous fifty-dollar tip to the bartender for his efforts.

Cheating and bluffing were commonplace for George Devol, an Ohio native who recorded many of his riverboat escapades in his 1887 autobiography, *Forty Years a Gambler on the Mississippi*.

Though he is known as the greatest Mississippi riverboat gambler in history, he was also a con artist and master of manipulation.

Born on August 1, 1829, in Marietta, Ohio, George Howard Devol was the youngest of six children. His father, Barker Devol, worked with his own father, Revolutionary War veteran Jonathan Devol, in a shipbuilding business. Since George's father frequently traveled for work, the youngest member of the family became a fun-loving troublemaker who constantly got into mischief and fights.

Living by the river, George couldn't resist the lure of the riverboats. At the tender age of ten, he climbed aboard the *Wacousta*, secured a job as a cabin boy, and left home without a word to his family. He soon discovered he could nearly double his pay from four to seven dollars a month on a ship called the *Walnut Hills*. But it was on the *Cicero* that George was introduced to a deck of playing cards. Working on the boat, he came to admire the gamblers who plied their trade onboard. A quick learner, he began his education in the fine art of card playing by observation, paying particular attention to the tricks of the trade.

George continued to hone his gambling skills, learning tips from seasoned gamblers. When the Mexican War broke out in 1846, he decided to fight in the war. To obtain free passage to Mexico, he found a position as a barkeeper on the *Corvette* as it headed toward the Rio Grande. But he soon discovered that cheating all the soldiers at cards was much more profitable than fighting a war.

By the time he returned to Ohio, George Devol was not quite seventeen years old and had about twenty-seven hundred dollars in his pocket from gambling. After showering his family with gifts at his homecoming, he decided to stay in Marietta and attempt to earn an honest living. For the next few years, George worked alongside his brother Paul, caulking steamboats. But George still couldn't resist the allure of gambling. As he explained in his autobiography, "Every Monday morning I went to work broke. I became infatuated with the game of faro, and it kept me a slave."

He also missed his old life on the riverboats. Finally, at the end of a hard day of work, George shoved his tools into the river and announced that "it was the last lick of work" he would ever do. When his brother asked about his future plans, George replied that he "intended to live off of fools and suckers."

George headed back to the riverboats, traveling up and down the Mississippi and becoming a master of gambling. Within a few years he garnered the reputation of a man who would never back down from a fight, a man who could outwit even the most experienced gamblers, and a man who was not above swindling anyone to win a hefty wager. By age thirty George had made hundreds of thousands of dollars working southern riverboats.

Weighing over two hundred pounds, he often had to rely on his physical prowess to defend himself from angry losers at the gaming tables. He claimed his hands were so large that he could "hold one deck in the palm of my hand and shuffle up another." But George also had a secret weapon that few men possessed: a hard head. As he explained, "I don't know . . . just how thick my old skull is; but I do know it must be pretty thick, or it would have been cracked many years ago, for I have been struck some terrible blows on my head . . . which would have split any man's skull wide open unless it was pretty thick."

Though George packed a revolver he called "Betsy Jane," his head was so hard that his primary weapon of defense was butting heads. One of his former victims explained, "The first lick he hit me, I thought my neck was disjointed; and when he ran that head into me, I thought it was a cannon ball." Another man admitted that he had been in a great many fights, but George Devol was the first man who had ever whipped him. When he had been head-butted by George, he felt like he had been struck with a bar of iron. No one fought that way where he came from, the man insisted, and the fight was far from fair. A member of the ship's crew reminded George's victim that everything was fair in a rough-and-tumble fight.

George often bragged about his encounter with William Carroll, a circus performer billed as "the man with the thick skull, or the great butter" who could out-butt anything in the show except the elephant. During a night of drinking in New Orleans, friends challenged the two men to see who could out-butt the other. George rammed his forehead into the man, who promptly saw stars. "Gentlemen," the man announced, "I have found my papa at last."

In spite of George's physical abilities to defend himself, he sometimes had to hide or escape from irate gamblers. On one occasion he overheard several victims conspiring to kill him and take back the money they had lost to him. George hid near the pilothouse and bribed the boat's pilot to veer the vessel close to the riverbank so he could jump off. As soon as he hit the water, George found himself trapped to the waist by the muddy bottom of the Mississippi River. His angry victims, realizing he had jumped ship, aimed their pistols and fired in his direction. Fortunately the steamboat picked up speed, and soon George was beyond the range of gunfire. Hearing the gunfire, a group of slaves came to his rescue and pulled him out of the river with a long pole. George remained on the riverbank until another steamboat stopped to pick him up.

George even donned disguises to escape the wrath of men he had fleeced. One day his victims became drunk and vowed to find the man who had fleeced them so they could recoup their losses. George put on some dirty clothes, smeared grime over his face, and joined the boat's roustabouts on the main deck. As soon as the boat docked at the next stop, he fell in with the other roustabouts as they hauled freight ashore. Meanwhile, his victims were still searching for him on the upper decks of the steamboat.

In another instance George overheard some men discussing how they could get back their money from him. They assumed he would try to get off the ship at the next stop and decided "to fill his hide full of lead if he tries that." As soon as the boat's whistle signaled to land, the men raced down to the lower deck, pistols in hand, to wait for George's exit. George slipped back to his cabin and donned a fine suit of clothes, a white necktie, a pair of gold glasses, and a bowler hat—and walked right through the group of men without being detected. "You would have bet five hundred bucks I was a preacher. You ought to have seen those fellows make room for me to pass by," George later recalled.

George even employed other people to help him leave the impression of being someone other than a gambler. He often pretended to be a plantation owner with rich pockets who had plenty to risk in a poker game. To help validate his claims, he even hired black men to carry his bags aboard the riverboat. During one hasty exit George recalled that the black slaves at a sugar plantation confirmed his false claims by greeting him at the wharf and exclaiming, "Glad youse back, Massa George."

During the Civil War, George had no remorse in bilking soldiers out of their payroll. "Paymasters in the Army were among the best suckers we had," he explained, especially drunk paymasters. By 1862 George had cheated soldiers out of so much money that the military governor of New Orleans, General Benjamin Franklin Butler, was forced to find a provost judge who would be willing to sentence him to a year in prison.

Even behind bars George continued his cheating ways, fleecing the other prisoners out of their money while in jail. Then he used the winnings to bribe his jailer into chaperoning him around the red-light district. He even bribed Louisiana governor George Shepley to pardon him. The governor agreed on the condition that he refrain from playing cards with any member of the Union Army. True to character George promptly broke his promise by bilking another paymaster out of nineteen thousand dollars. And he remained in business another two years until a wise general closed Southern gambling houses to protect the payroll.

"After cheating all the soldiers I could at cards," George returned his focus to civilians. Even ministers were not immune to George's swindling ways. On one trip from New Orleans to Louisville, George played games throughout the night in the barbershop. The next morning he met a minister who insisted that George listen to the sermon that he planned to deliver onboard the riverboat. During the sermon the minister mentioned he had stayed awake for most of the night due to the noisy card game in the onboard barbershop. Though the minister did not look directly at George, the gambler knew the message was intended for him.

Later that evening he ran into the minister again. When the
man of the cloth began to berate the gambling games of the previous evening, George insisted he had been roped into the game.
He'd lost one thousand dollars, he lied smoothly, but his rich father
had footed the bill.

The minister asked lots of questions about gambling, then
asked to see how one of the games was played. George demonstrated
three-card monte, explaining that the dealer places three cards face
down, then reveals one of the cards as the "target card." He rear-
ranges the cards quickly to confuse the player about which card
is which. The player then has the chance to pick one of the three
cards. If the player correctly identifies the target card, he wins.

The minister practiced the games a few times, then said, "My
dear sir, I can't see how you could lose money on such a simple
thing. I would not fail to pick out the right ticket every time."
George proposed that they play a hand for two hundred dollars,
and the winner would donate the money to the minister's church.

The minister agreed. Within moments he had lost five hands
to the tune of one thousand dollars. George gave the minister one
more chance. "I will put up the one thousand dollars against your
watch and chain, and when you gain it back we can have a big
laugh over it," the gambler offered. With one more flip of the cards,
the minister turned over his belongings to George.

The next morning George went to the minister's cabin and
found the man on his knees in prayer. When the minister revealed
he had been praying for both himself and George, the gambler
returned the minister's money, watch, and chain. "Go, and sin no
more," George advised.

But more than one minister became trapped in the gambler's
hold. "I caught a preacher once for all his money, his gold spec-
tacles, and his sermons," George wrote in his memoirs, adding
that he returned "his sermons and specks"—but not his money.
On another evening George played monte with fifteen preachers
headed to a conference. He later boasted that he took five of the
men for every cent they had. "Preachers are but human, and some

of them will steal the livery of the court of heaven to serve the devil," he noted.

Despite his love of fighting and reputation as being hardheaded, there was a soft side to George Devol. In *Forty Years a Gambler* he recounts meeting a young widow at a dance onboard the *Magnolia*. Instantly smitten with "the most agreeable and sweetest woman I had ever met in my life," George was thrilled when she invited him to her plantation. During a three-day visit to her home, he fell madly in love with the woman. They met again on several occasions, and the widow begged George to quit gambling and settle down. She also invited him for another visit to the plantation. "I have often thought what a different man I might have been if I had accepted that last invitation," he wrote thirty years later.

He also despised men who stole from their wives to support their gambling habits. After one man lost a few hundred dollars at the table, he returned to his cabin with the keys to his wife's trunk. He retrieved some jewelry and a fine shawl from the trunk, sold the items to a passenger, took the money back to the gaming tables, and promptly lost all of it. When George learned about the situation, he found the buyer of the goods, purchased the items, and returned them to the wife. "I advised her to keep her keys from her husband, and have no doubt she was very grateful to me for it, for she seemed to be. I did not want the lady to lose her jewelry and shawl," he said.

George even had a soft spot for the less fortunate. When he encountered a woman who did not have the funds to travel on the *Natchez* with her six children, George passed his top hat among the passengers and crew at the dock. Everyone contributed to the cause except for one man. George took the hatful of bank notes and silver coins to the captain to pay the passage for the woman and her children. The captain, however, refused to take the money and instructed George to give the funds to the woman. He also made arrangements to book the family into a stateroom and treat them as if they had paid the full first-class fare.

George presented the money to the woman and headed to the saloon. When he opened a game of three-card monte, the man who had declined to put anything into the collection for the woman was one of the first players to join in the game. To the delight of everyone in the saloon, the man lost eight hundred dollars to George. One of the observers even taunted the man by asking, "Aren't you sorry you didn't give something to the woman before you lost your money?"

After the Civil War George headed west, traveling in posh railroad cars and gambling along the way. By his own account, he fleeced everyone from cowpokes to miners in places like Kansas City and Cheyenne. He also rubbed shoulders with the rich and famous. While gambling in the Gold Room Saloon in Cheyenne, Wyoming, he met the infamous Wild Bill Hickok. And while traveling the Cheyenne-to-Omaha route aboard the Missouri Railroad, he unknowingly gambled with the director of the railroad.

In spite of his hard-headed nature and penchant for winning, George claimed he never took money from a friend during all his years of gambling. Moreover, he insisted he always checked with the clerk on every riverboat to make certain that his victims had enough money to get home. In 1892 George published his autobiography, *Forty Years a Gambler on the Mississippi*. By the time he retired from professional gambling in 1896, George Howard Devol was sixty-seven years old. He claimed he had won more than two million dollars in his forty years of gambling, estimated to be about fifty million in today's dollars. But he had lost most of his winnings to dealers who were even more crooked than he. "My old head is hard and thick, and maybe that is the reason I never had sense enough to save my money. It is said of me that I have won more money than any sporting man in this country," he wrote in his autobiography. "I will say that I hadn't sense enough to keep it."

George spent the last few years of his life hawking his memoirs. He died in Hot Springs, Arkansas, in 1903, but the King of the Riverboat Gamblers was nearly penniless, never recouping the millions that he had won and lost.

Nancy Farrer

Insane Poisoner or Witless Dupe?
1832–185?

When Nancy Farrer was escorted into the Court of Common Pleas for Hamilton County, Ohio, jurors and curious spectators stared in disbelief. Though the stout woman appeared composed, her homely features were so disdainful that the throng of onlookers couldn't help but gape at the sight.

Cruel observers labeled her as "the ugliest girl ever known in Cincinnati." One eyewitness noted that she was an "object of horror that prejudged her from the first" with "the repulsive plainness and brutality of her face." Judging solely by her looks, the public had already condemned her for fatally poisoning young James Wesley Forest during the brief time she worked in his family's home as a domestic servant.

On that cold February day in 1852, Nancy Farrer seemed to be doomed for execution. Even though the proceedings had not yet begun, everyone in the courtroom assumed she was plainly incompetent.

During an investigation of the murder, Nancy's extraordinary facial features had been the topic of debate among medical experts. "The most remarkable point was the distance between her eyebrows, across the bridge of her nose, being about four times as great as in any ordinary person. Many [medical experts] considered it as positive proof that she was demented," explained Dr. J. J. Quinn, who wrote about Nancy's case in 1855 for the *Western Lancet: A Monthly Journal of Practical Medicine and Surgery*. Other medical experts concluded that her deformed features did not necessarily interfere with her reason and believed she had a sound mind.

Nancy Farrer
WESTERN LANCET: A MONTHLY JOURNAL OF PRACTICAL MEDICINE AND SURGERY, VOL. 16.

But Nancy's attorney did not share the opinion of medical experts. Young Rutherford B. Hayes, appointed by the judge of the criminal court to conduct Nancy's defense, intended to save his client from execution by winning the case on the grounds of insanity. "There is no fact more essential to crime than the possession of reason," he wrote in his diary.

By tradition, courts had long turned to medical experts to determine if a prisoner was insane. Though everyone agreed that an insane person is not morally responsible for a criminal act, the medical determination of a person's insanity was based on the prisoner's ability to recognize right from wrong.

The young defense attorney studied the subject of insanity in relationship to criminal acts. In his diary he quoted a profound thought attributed to Dr. Luther V. Bell, who had been appointed superintendent of the McLean Asylum outside Boston in 1826. "I consider that insane persons *generally* know the difference between right and wrong," Dr. Bell stated. This statement became the centerpiece of Rutherford's arguments in the defense of Nancy Farrer.

The future president of the United States also realized that the case would be a notable trial that presented an opportunity to launch his career. "It is the criminal case of the term" that "will attract more notice than any other," he penned in another diary entry. Moreover, he stated, "If I am well prepared will give me a better opportunity to exert and exhibit whatever pith there is in me than any case I ever appeared in."

Rutherford Hayes must have also realized that the pitiful Nancy Farrer desperately needed his help. Sound reasoning, good judgment, and family stability had been absent from Nancy's life since she was born in Lancashire County, England, in July 1832. She and her mother emigrated to the United States in about 1844, two years after her father and younger brother had arrived in America. The family lived in Nauvoo, Illinois, for two years before relocating to Cincinnati, where her father may have practiced his trade as a cobbler.

Most likely the influence of Nancy's mother and father psychologically damaged their daughter. Her father attempted suicide on two occasions and eventually died from the effects of alcoholism at the Commercial Hospital of Cincinnati in 1847. Her mother, a religious fanatic who claimed to be a Mormon prophetess and "the bride of Christ," was considered to be insane.

Lacking skills and an education, Nancy began working as a domestic servant in the homes of several Cincinnati residents during her teen years. By November 1851 she was living in the household of Elisha Forest, cleaning, cooking, and tending to daily chores for the family.

Elisha's wife, who was already gravely ill, died within a week of Nancy's arrival. On November 20, about two weeks after the death of Mrs. Forest, the youngest member of the family, two-year-old John Edward Forest, suddenly became violently ill. He died the following day. The same debilitating illness struck Elisha and his eldest son, Billy, during the last part of November, but both recovered from the mysterious illness.

The final fatal tragedy for the Forest family came on December 1, 1851, with the death of James Wesley Forest. The child was only eight years old. An autopsy revealed the presence of arsenic in the boy's stomach.

Initially the case baffled investigators. The Forests were respected members of the community, with no known enemies. Who could be responsible for three deaths in the same family within one month? Suddenly all eyes focused on Nancy. All the deaths had occurred since her arrival in the household.

Then police learned that another woman, a Mrs. Green, and her young daughter, Annie, had also died mysteriously while Nancy was employed in their home earlier in the year. To connect the missing pieces of the mystery, officials ordered the exhumation of the bodies of Mrs. Green and Mrs. Forest, along with the two Forest boys. In each instance the cause of death was arsenic poisoning. Investigators also discovered that Nancy Farrer had purchased arsenic from several local drugstores within recent months.

Police arrested their prime suspect and charged her with first-degree murder in the death of her latest victim, James Wesley Forest. While waiting for her murder trial to begin, Nancy was locked up in the county jail.

According to one historical source, a mysterious man persuaded Nancy Farrer to commit the crimes. He then skipped town and left Nancy to take the sole blame for the murders. As Dr. Quinn explained, Nancy was "wholly in the power of the man who insti-gated her crimes. . . . Once under the sway of the real murderer, who had won the wretched creature's love in order the better to enslave her will, she had no volition of her own." The mysterious man, how-ever, played no role in determining Nancy's guilt in the trial.

On opening day of the trial, the courthouse was packed with onlookers who were captivated by the deformed features of the woman accused of murder. Throughout the trial Nancy's face bore a silly impression, and she was easily distracted by sudden noises or movements in the courtroom. She actually seemed indifferent to the proceedings that would determine if she would be executed or walk free from the courtroom. To the most casual observer, the woman's intellectual abilities appeared to be very low.

But as Rutherford B. Hayes began his argument to save his client's life, both the jurors and spectators shifted their attention to the eloquent words of the young attorney. Rutherford freely con-ceded that Nancy Farrer had poisoned the little boy. But he also persuaded the jury to consider that Nancy was "not a morally free agent," even though she knew the difference between right and wrong. And he pleaded with the jury on a deeply personal level:

> *The calamity of insanity is one which may touch very nearly the happiness of the best of our citizens. We all know that in some of its thousand forms, it has carried grief and agony unspeakable into many a happy home; and we must all wish to see such rules in regard to it established as would satisfy an intelligent man if, instead of this friendless girl, his own sister or his own daughter were on trial. And surely to establish such rules will be a most noble achievement of that intelligence and reason which God has given to you, but died to her whose fate is in your hands.*

Testimonies and arguments lasted nine days. After sixty-three hours of deliberation, the jurors returned to the Court of Common

Pleas on February 18, 1852, and announced a verdict of guilty for murder in the first degree. In spite of the brilliant defense attorney's arguments, the jurors still believed that the girl was answerable for her crime if she knew right from wrong. A motion for a new trial was overruled, and Nancy Farrer was sentenced to death by hanging on June 25, 1852.

But Rutherford Hayes continued the fight to save Nancy's life. As she awaited execution in the county jail, the attorney filed a "writ of error" with the Ohio Supreme Court. The request asked the higher court to review the records of the original trial for errors committed during the proceedings. The state supreme court accepted the request and scheduled a review for December 1853, nearly two years after Nancy's original conviction. Her execution was delayed indefinitely.

Once again Rutherford presented a passionate, logical plea for his client. When he finished the argument, one of the judges proclaimed it was "the best first speech" he had ever heard in the Ohio Supreme Court. The motion for a new trial was granted.

But a new trial did not take place. At an inquest of lunacy, Rutherford Hayes managed to persuade the court that Nancy Farrer was not responsible for her actions—even though she knew they were wrong—simply because she could not help herself. The court agreed with the attorney's argument and ruled that his client was of "unsound mind," setting a precedent in the determination of insanity for future court decisions. After the ruling Nancy was removed from the county jail and sent to the Hamilton County Lunatic Asylum.

On the day that the results of the inquest were revealed, Rutherford recorded his thoughts in his diary. "She will now go to a lunatic asylum, and so my first case involving life is ended successfully," he wrote. "It has been a pet case with me; has caused me much anxiety, given me some prominence in my profession. It has turned out fortunately for me—very, and I am greatly gratified that it is so."

Dr. J. J. Quinn, superintendent of the Hamilton County Lunatic Asylum, reported in his *Western Lancet* article that Nancy had adjusted well to her new home "and appears to be perfectly satisfied with her situation." She was remarkably cheerful, neat, and kind, according to Dr. Quinn, who claimed "she is one of the best hands there." He also observed that Nancy could speak rationally on any subject, and was respectful and truthful in her dealings with other inmates and the staff. "The keepers all assert that they have yet to see the first signs of insanity," and the "closest scrutiny has been unable to detect the least evidence of mental weakness of intellectual or moral impairment," he reported.

Perhaps Nancy found a form of stability within the walls of the lunatic asylum that she had never known, a stability that calmed her inner demons. But not even Dr. Quinn could predict how she might respond to living in another environment. "How, or in what manner, a life in society under other circumstances and other influences would affect these traits in her character, can only be a matter of conjecture," he said.

Still, even the doctor could not fully associate the heartless murders with the kind young woman under his care. "It is difficult to reconcile the poisoning of so many innocent and harmless persons, with her amiable, kindhearted and affectionate disposition, without supposing the presence, at the time, of an irrational motive, or insane impulse," he wrote in his article.

Nancy Farrer died of unknown causes in the Hamilton County Lunatic Asylum after living in the institution for only a few years. The motivations for poisoning her victims, however, will forever remain a mystery. "It is probable that her designs for perpetrating her wholesale murders will ever remain locked up in her own bosom, and that she will carry to the grave the secrets of her mysterious doings," Dr. Quinn surmised.

Victoria Claflin Woodhull

Scandalous Suffragette
1838–1927

On November 20, 1871, a fashionably dressed, attractive woman with bright blue eyes stepped up to the podium at Steinway Hall in New York City. An audience of three thousand people sat in the concert hall, eagerly waiting to hear Victoria Claflin Woodhull speak on "The Principles of Social Freedom."

As Victoria spoke about the changing attitudes toward social freedom, the crowd applauded often and vigorously. But as she reached the part of the speech on women's rights, she veered from her prepared notes and spoke from the heart. "It has been my province to study 'free love' in all its various lights and shades. . . . can see no moral difference between a woman who marries and lives with a man because he can provide for her wants and the woman who is not married but who is provided for at the same price. . . . The sexual relation must be rescued from this insidious form of slavery."

"Mrs. Woodhull, are *you* a free lover?" a heckler shouted.

Victoria tossed her prepared speech to the floor and directly addressed the audience. "Yes, I am a free lover," she proclaimed defiantly. "I have an inalienable, constitutional and natural right to love whom I may; to love as long or as short a period as I can; to change that love every day if I please."

The crowd went wild, drowning out anything more Victoria might have said. In the days that followed, newspapers reprinted her radical remarks. Shocked by Victoria's statements, readers denounced her. To her supporters she became known as "Queen Victoria." To her enemies she was known as "Mrs. Satan."

Victoria Claflin Woodhull

In the late nineteenth century, American culture embraced the standards of the Victorian era with its high moral values, strict social code of conduct, and sexual restraint. But Victoria Woodhull defied the acceptable moral standards of the day by pushing the limits of appropriate behavior and traditional beliefs of the times. The shocking content of Victoria's speeches and articles about "free love" and news of her unorthodox lifestyle rocked the nation during the last half of the nineteenth century. Moreover, events that transpired in Woodhull's personal life were some of the most scandalous of the era.

Victoria's life, even from an early age, was anything but conventional. Born on September 23, 1838, in Homer, Ohio, she was the sixth of ten children born to Roxanne and Buck Claflin. Roxanne, known as Anna, chose Victoria as the name for her baby in honor of the British monarch who had been crowned earlier that year.

The Claflins struggled to provide the basic necessities for the family and resorted to unconventional—and often illegal means— to earn money. A petty thief, counterfeiter, and con man, Claflin tried his hand at everything, from working in taverns to transporting lumber. But he found his greatest success in selling worthless concoctions that claimed to cure a variety of ailments through a traveling medicine show. Anna, a religious zealot who claimed to be a clairvoyant, sold her services as a fortune-teller.

From an early age Victoria attended religious prayer meetings with her mother. Though she had only three years of formal education, the intelligent young girl quickly picked up on the spiritual messages and was soon warning other children to repent of their sins. Youngsters seemed enthralled by Victoria's convincing arguments. Recognizing a moneymaking opportunity in his daughter's talents for public speaking, Claflin began to market her services as a child clairvoyant and fortune-teller in his traveling show.

The residents of the small town of Homer disdained Claflin and his underhanded ways. Around 1853 Claflin was suspected of burning his old gristmill to collect five hundred dollars in insurance money. Hearing that enraged neighbors had set out to find him, Claflin fled town, leaving behind his wife and children. Though residents were unprepared and unwilling to support the Claflin clan, the Presbyterian Church in Homer raised enough money to buy a horse-drawn wagon and supplies for Anna and the children. Then they promptly asked the family to leave town.

The family caught up with Claflin in Mount Gilead, Ohio, a short distance from Homer, at the home of the Claflin's eldest daughter, Margaret Ann, her husband, Enos Miles, and their three children.

Still needing income to support his family, Claflin looked to two of his young daughters for help. From an early age Victoria believed she could communicate with the dead and heal the sick. Her younger sister, Tennessee Claflin, also possessed unexplainable abilities to predict the future. At the tender age of five, Tennie, as she was called, had predicted a fire with such precision that she was suspected of setting the blaze.

Once again exploiting his children, Claflin advertised the services of his daughters as mediums for one dollar per visit. At the time, Victoria was fourteen years old, and Tennie was only seven. Working as fortune-tellers, the girls soon became the family's primary means of support.

While living in Mount Gilead, Victoria caught the eye of a local doctor, Canning Woodhull. At age twenty-eight, he was nearly twice the age of Victoria. After a short romance the two were married on November 23, 1853, one month after Victoria's fifteenth birthday.

Wedded bliss, however, was not part of the couple's marriage. Victoria soon realized that her groom spent most of his money on spirits. Dr. Woodhull had only a few patients and very little money. Along with his alcoholism, Woodhull abused his wife, even after she became pregnant with their first child. Their son, Bryan, born one year after the couple exchanged vows, was mentally unstable. Some historians contend that the child may have had a form of mental retardation that could be attributed to Woodhull kicking Victoria in the stomach during her pregnancy. Victoria, who often referred to her son as an imbecile, blamed Bryan's retardation on her husband's alcoholism.

Trapped in a loveless marriage, Victoria's dreams of happiness were shattered. "I supposed that to marry was to be transported to a heaven not only of happiness but of purity and perfection. . . . But, alas, how were my beliefs dispelled! . . . I soon learned that what I had believed of marriage and society was the nearest sham."

Worse yet, Victoria came to realize that marriage meant a woman was under legal bondage to her husband. Her body, her wealth, and her children were his property. Women had few, if any, opportunities to gain financial independence and were totally dependent on their husbands for economic security. This stark realization became the foundation of her beliefs in the doctrine of free love and equal rights for women.

In 1861 Victoria gave birth to a daughter, Zulu Maude. This time she felt blessed with the gift of a healthy, happy child. But unlike most women, Victoria knew she could not rely on her husband to support the family. Defying conventional standards, she took matters into her own hands and teamed up with Tennie to conduct spiritual readings and healings.

She also decided she could no longer tolerate her husband's alcoholism and abusive ways. In 1864, following eleven years of marriage to Woodhull, she filed for divorce—an extraordinary and rare occurrence during the era.

Meanwhile, Victoria and Tennie set up shop in Cincinnati as clairvoyants and found financial success beyond their wildest dreams, making nearly one hundred thousand dollars in one year. But neighbors watching a parade of men enter the business grew suspicious of the type of medicine being practiced by the two sisters. Since society often considered mediums to be synonymous with prostitution, the sisters were asked to leave Cincinnati when neighbors claimed they were operating a brothel.

Victoria and Tennie relocated to Chicago for a brief time, but were evicted from the city for fraudulent fortune-telling. Deciding to "minister" to those who were suffering from the effects of the Civil War, the Claflin sisters joined the rest of the family to tour several states with their medical road show. By the time the Claflin caravan arrived in St. Louis, Missouri, in 1865, the group had made thousands of dollars hawking sham medicine and spirit communications throughout the war-torn South.

In St. Louis, Victoria set up in a hotel to exercise her powers. Among her customers was a Civil War veteran who was also a prominent local spiritualist. Fresh from the battlefield and scarred by five bullet wounds, Colonel James Harvey Blood sought Victoria's services as a spiritualistic physician. Shared interest in spiritualism and a mutual attraction for each other swiftly ignited a heated romance. Blood soon divorced his wife, and he and Victoria married in 1866.

Victoria and her new husband agreed that their partnership would be a marriage of equals, and Blood fully supported his bride's longing to fight for equal rights for women. Led by a spiritual guide, Blood, Victoria, and her two children moved to New York in 1868. A throng of Claflin relatives followed, including Victoria and Tennie's parents and two of their sisters, who brought their own families.

Though Victoria had planned to take up the fight for women's rights as soon as she arrived in New York, she quickly realized she needed funding to support her dreams. Her father, always ready to turn a quick buck, immediately launched a search for customers who could benefit from the talents of his daughters. He did not have to look far to find a wealthy, willing customer in need of their services: millionaire Cornelius Vanderbilt, often known as the Commodore.

It was no secret that Vanderbilt often consulted spiritualists to communicate with his deceased parents. He also preferred the services of "magnetic" healers, rather than medical doctors, to treat his physical ailments. These healers used their hands to supposedly magnetize the patient, using the touch of their hands like an electric prod to jolt the body back into shape.

The year 1868 had not been kind to the seventy-three-year-old shipping and railroad tycoon. His wife, Sophia, had died that year, and he had lost seven million dollars in a struggle over control of the Erie Railroad. Knowing of Vanderbilt's losses, Claflin knew that Victoria could help with his spiritual pursuits and Tennessee could care for his body. At age twenty-two, Tennessee was a precocious beauty who could work wonders on his aging body and sagging spirits with her magnetic powers. Victoria could use her powers as a clairvoyant to help predict stock market trends.

Vanderbilt agreed to hire the sisters, and he paid generously for their services. Finally, with financial resources in hand, Victoria launched her fight for women's rights. In January 1869 she traveled to Washington, DC, to attend the first National Woman Suffrage convention ever held in the nation's capital.

Victoria also took another step in the fight for equality by walking along a path that no woman had ever dared to walk. With financial backing from Cornelius Vanderbilt, Victoria and Tennie became the first female stockbrokers in American history. The sisters earned instant notoriety on February 5, 1870, when Woodhull, Claflin & Co. formally opened its doors to the public. The *New York Times* featured the women in a front-page story with the headline, "Petticoats Among the Bovine and Ursine Animals." News of a brokerage firm operated by women caused a frenzy of speculation at the stock and gold exchange, and an estimated four thousand visitors, primarily men, visited their offices at 44 Broad Street—on opening day.

Within a few months the sisters also launched a newspaper, *Woodhull & Claflin's Weekly*, a sixteen-page publication that would eventually boast of twenty thousand subscribers. The journal addressed controversial topics ranging from women's suffrage to stock swindles, insurance fraud, and corrupt congressional land deals. It was also the first American publication to reprint *The Communist Manifesto*.

But Victoria shrewdly planned to use the journal for personal purposes—primarily to publicize her campaign to run for president of the United States. Even though females did not have the right to vote, no laws prevented women from running from office. Victoria announced her plans to run for president in the *New York Herald* on April 2, 1870, becoming the first woman in American history to seek the office.

Her "firsts" as a female stockbroker and presidential candidate placed her in the national spotlight, and she added another "first" to her accomplishments on January 11, 1871. On that date Victoria became the first woman in history to address a committee of the US Congress when she appeared before the House Judiciary Committee to deliver a speech on women's suffrage. She pointed out to the committee that the fourteenth and fifteenth amendments granted the right to vote to all citizens. Since women were citizens, she argued, they already had the right to vote. Impressed by Victoria's speech, representatives of the National Woman Suffrage Association (NWSA) asked her to speak at their convention the next day.

With much of the national spotlight focused on Victoria, news of her unorthodox lifestyle grew expediently. Newspapers revealed that Victoria's first husband was living in the same house with her and her current husband. Was the divorced suffragette practicing the "free love" that she advocated? In reality Doctor Woodhull had shown up at Victoria's doorstep, penniless and addicted to morphine, and Victoria did not have the heart to turn away the father of her children.

Though she adamantly supported women's rights in both the boardroom and the bedroom, Victoria also detested society's double standard for men in terms of fidelity. Moreover, she was troubled by the discovery that the Reverend Henry Ward Beecher had been having an affair with Elizabeth Tilton, wife of Beecher's best friend, Theodore Tilton. Beecher was a fiery evangelical minister whose sermons often denounced sexual activity outside of marriage. Rumors swarmed through New York City about Beecher's numerous affairs with women in his parish. Some versions of the story even claimed he had several illegitimate children.

After Victoria had agreed to appear at Steinway Hall to speak on "The Principles of Social Freedom" on November 20, 1871, she urged the reverend to introduce her. When he refused to answer her written appeals, she threatened to expose his affair with Elizabeth Tilton.

Eleven months later Victoria followed through on her threat to expose Beecher's infidelities to the world by featuring "The Beecher-Tilton Scandal Case" in the *Woodhull & Claflin Weekly.* The same issue also contained information on a shameless New York stockbroker who had boasted about molesting innocent teen girls. By the end of the week, demand was so high for the publication that the issue was reprinted. Copies sold at forty dollars each.

The scandalous stories shocked the nation. Within days Victoria and Tennessee were arrested on charges of sending obscene material through the mail. On November 5, 1872, the presidential election day that should have been a milestone for Victoria, the scandalous suffragette was sitting in a New York City jail.

In the following months Victoria and Tennessee were sued for criminal libel and endured weeks of imprisonment in more than one jail. The sisters ultimately paid about a half million dollars in fines and bail, including sixty thousand dollars for an alleged misdemeanor. Although they were eventually found innocent of all charges, the government confiscated their printing press, personal papers, and brokerage accounts.

Though bankrupt and discredited, Victoria continued to give speeches on free love and women's rights. Speaking to a group of spiritualists on August 17, 1873, she compared marriage to slavery, proclaiming:

> *You are the sexual slaves of your husbands, bound by as terrible bonds to serve them sexually as ever a negro was bound to serve his owner, physically; and if you don't believe it, go home and endeavor to assert your freedom . . . lashes of some sort will surely be dealt . . . even to compelling you*

to submit by force. . . . All the suffering of all the negro slaves combined is as nothing in comparison to that which women, as a whole, suffer.

In 1875 Theodore Tilton sued Reverend Beecher for willfully alienating himself from the affections of his wife. The lawsuit ignited a sensational trial, but Victoria managed not to testify during the proceedings. The following year she ceased publication of *Woodhull & Claflin's Weekly*, and she filed for divorce from Colonel Blood.

Another issue of potential controversy with the Claflin sisters occurred in 1877 with the death of Cornelius Vanderbilt. One of the Commodore's sons, William, apparently had no desire for anyone to discover the sordid details about the sisters' relationship with his father. In the middle of a legal dispute about his father's will, William approached the sisters with a generous offer. In exchange for leaving the country, he was prepared to offer them more than one hundred thousand dollars.

It was an offer they could not refuse. Victoria and Tennie were soon living in England. Pleased with the reception and acceptance of the British, Victoria once again hit the lecture circuit. Her speeches, however, took a more subtle approach than her emotional outbursts in America. "Free love is not what I asked for nor what I pleaded for. What I asked for was educated love, that our daughters be taught to love rightly."

At a London lecture hall, Victoria met John B. Martin, a wealthy London banker and heir to a large estate. In the fall of 1883, the couple married. They took great pains to mend Victoria's American reputation, attempting to claim blood relations to the founding fathers of the United States. The couple also filed libel charges against the British Museum in early 1894 for allowing pamphlets discussing the Beecher-Tilton trial to be open to public view. They claimed these pamphlets were incriminating to Woodhull's character because of false information. Though they did not win the case, they made it clear that they did not want Victoria's name used in any way that would harm her reputation.

Victoria and her third husband purchased and lived in a mansion in Hyde Park, an elegant neighborhood in London. Tennessee also married into prestige and money, becoming the wife of Francis Cook. She became a proper English lady and one of the wealthiest people in England.

In 1892 Victoria began publishing the *Humanitarian, a Monthly Magazine of Sociology*. She researched and wrote on a range of issues from politics to food safety. In the same year, Victoria and her husband traveled to New York City and launched the United States' version of the magazine.

After fourteen years of marriage to Victoria, Martin died at age fifty-five. He left his assets to his wife, including his family's land in Bredon's Norton, a small town outside London. Following his death, Victoria moved to the estate and used her money to gain favor with the people of Bredon's Norton. Initially some residents protested her gifts by smashing gaslights that she had donated to the town. But Victoria managed to create a positive identity for herself by giving away much of the land she had inherited and presenting the region with many generous donations.

In her later years Victoria became an automobile enthusiast and one of the first women to drive from England through France and back. At age sixty-five she became a proud member of the Ladies Automobile Club and helped organize the Women's Aerial League of Great Britain to promote the joys of airplanes.

Victoria died on June 9, 1927, in London at age eighty-eight. Though she desperately tried to restore respect to her name while living in England, her reputation in America remained tarnished. The Ohio native made history with a number of "firsts" for a woman in the United States, but her scandalous beliefs and lifestyle overshadowed most of her accomplishments.

Stephen Wallace Dorsey

Senator and Swindler
1842–1916

When Stephen Wallace Dorsey stepped into his seat in the United States Senate on March 3, 1873, as a first-term senator from Arkansas, allegations of bribery were already swirling around the recent Ohio transplant. By December 1874 the Arkansas General Assembly had launched an investigation about the bribery charges, stating:

> *Whereas, it has long been currently reported, and almost universally believed, that Senator Dorsey procured his election to the United States Senate by corrupt appliances and bribery. Therefore:*
> *Be it resolved by the Senate, the House concurring, that a joint committee . . . be raised for the purpose of investigating the matter by what appliances, Mr. Dorsey, a stranger, unknown to the people of Arkansas, secured his election to the high and responsible office of United States senator.*

The Arkansas political investigation was not the first time that Stephen Dorsey had been accused of corruption, nor would it be the last. Throughout his successful political and business career, he was repeatedly accused of wielding his power and influence for personal financial gain through a multitude of unscrupulous schemes and scandals.

Stephen Wallace Dorsey was born on a farm in Benson, Vermont, located in rural Rutland County, on February 28, 1842. He was the seventh of ten children born to Irish immigrants John and

Stephen Wallace Dorsey
COURTESY, LIBRARY OF CONGRESS, LC-DIG-CWPBH-00500

Mary Dorsey. Since the Dorseys were devout Congregationalists, Stephen attended the denomination's schools. John Dorsey died when Stephen was nine years old, and the youngster left home by the time he was fifteen.

After finding employment as a farmer for a brief time in Minnesota, Stephen joined a community of Vermont transplants in

Oberlin, Ohio. Working as a house painter, he lived in the household of the Oberlin postmaster, Chauncey Wack.

In August 1861, at age nineteen, Dorsey joined Ohio's Battery H of the First Regiment Light Artillery at Fort Dennison, near Cincinnati. The artillery unit played a strategic role in major battles throughout the Civil War, and Dorsey advanced to the rank of major. In October 1867 he was commissioned as a lieutenant colonel, receiving the postwar honor "for gallant and meritorious services at the battle of Wilderness, Spotsylvania, Cold Harbor, and Petersburg, Virginia." Years later, in the midst of the scandals that constantly surrounded Dorsey, his supporters would note that his bravery on the battlefield exemplified his strong character. Extremely proud of his military service, Dorsey was a lifelong member of the Grand Army of the Republic.

Dorsey mustered out of the army at Cleveland, Ohio, in June 1864, and immediately returned to Oberlin. Five months later he married Helen Mary Wack, a raven-haired beauty who was known as "the prettiest girl in Oberlin." Stephen had become acquainted with Helen while living in her father's household before the war.

After a brief move to Alabama, he and his wife settled in Sandusky, Ohio, where he took a job in a tool factory. By 1869 he and two friends had established the Sandusky Tool Company, and Dorsey was named superintendent of the business. The company prospered by manufacturing garden tools and precise woodworking tools. Sandusky tools became famous throughout the country and are still highly valued by woodworkers today.

In 1869 the Dorseys expanded the size of their family with the birth of a daughter, Carlotta, who was often called "Lottie." Their second child, Clayton Chauncey Dorsey, was born in Sandusky two years later.

While residing in Sandusky, Dorsey also became active in local Republican politics. He was elected to the Sandusky City Council and later selected as a delegate to the Ohio State Republican convention that nominated Ulysses S. Grant for president. Not yet thirty years old, Dorsey was already establishing a name for himself as a successful politician and businessman.

With his talents and impressive track record in business, Dorsey was soon elected president of the Arkansas Central Railway Company. In this position he was expected to build rail track from Helena to Little Rock, Arkansas. Since legislation allowed railroad companies to sell government-backed bonds to finance expansion projects, Dorsey was issued bonds for more than $1.5 million. After selling most of the bonds, he had enough money to start building the railroad line in 1871.

Dorsey packed up his family and moved from Ohio to Helena, Arkansas, located in Phillips County. By 1872 forty-eight miles of the railway were opened from Helena to Clarendon, but the project stalled before the rails reached Little Rock. Dorsey claimed he was unable to sell all the bonds and was forced to mortgage the railroad for money to continue construction.

Rumors soon surfaced that large sums of money had vanished from the Arkansas Central Railway, sparking the first scandal of Dorsey's career. Allegations also arose of Dorsey bribing certain officials. Moreover, the actual building expenses were less than the total amount of the bonds, with the railroad administration—meaning Dorsey himself—pocketing the difference. Some historians contend that Dorsey made between sixty and seventy thousand dollars on the deal.

Word of the scandal soon hit the press. The *Daily Arkansas Gazette* described Dorsey as "a man of fair ability, indifferently honest as times go, having never been caught stealing anything bigger than a railroad."

Despite his railroad's financial problems, Dorsey set his sights on a political career in Washington. Arkansas senator Benjamin Rice was stepping down from his post, and Dorsey was determined to become the next junior senator from Arkansas. Since the new senator would be elected by the state's General Assembly, Dorsey focused his efforts on wooing votes from the state legislature.

Once again scandal erupted around Dorsey. As the *New York*

Times reported, "Charges of treachery and bribery flew thick and fast and money flowed like water. It was said that the members were bought like bundles of merchandise, some of it money from Arkansas Central Railroad bonds."

In spite of the controversy swirling around him, Dorsey won the election and took his seat in the US Senate on March 4, 1873. The Arkansas General Assembly named a newly established county in honor of Dorsey during the year of his election to the US Senate. In 1885 the name was changed to Cleveland County in honor of US President Grover Cleveland.

Twenty months after Dorsey took the oath of office in the US Senate, the Arkansas General Assembly held hearings of a joint house-senate committee to investigate the allegations of bribery. Witnesses provided damaging statements, especially Arkansas governor Elisha Baxter, who testified that Dorsey had "suggested" that he had forty thousand dollars to spend on the election.

But the General Assembly could not find a paper trail of written checks to prove that bribery had taken place. With hearsay as the only evidence, Dorsey walked away unscathed by the charges, escaping censure and possible impeachment.

On a national scale, an economic crisis hit the country about the same time that Dorsey arrived in Washington. During the financial panic of 1873, banks failed across the nation, and industrial development and railroad construction came to a virtual standstill. The Arkansas Central Railway Company did not escape the crisis, failing to meet its interest payments. By 1875 Dorsey was forced to file personal bankruptcy in the Western District Court at Helena, Arkansas.

During his term in the US Senate, Dorsey proposed one piece of legislation that still impacts Americans today. The junior senator from Arkansas introduced a bill to add the birthdate of President George Washington as the fifth official bank holiday observance. Congress had previously approved four official bank holidays: New Year's Day, Independence Day, Thanksgiving, and Christmas Day.

When Dorsey's senate term ended on March 3, 1879, he did

not run for reelection. However, he remained active for some time in national politics. When the Republicans nominated James G. Garfield for president and Chester A. Arthur for vice president in 1880, Dorsey became the secretary of the Republican National Committee. He had been named as a member of the Republican National Committee during his term in the senate.

Shortly before leaving the senate, Dorsey traveled to New Mexico in search of new adventures and to purchase land with the intent of relocating to the state once he had completed his senatorial obligations. In 1878, he started building a lavish Victorian mansion in the Mountain Springs area of Colfax County, New Mexico. After two years of construction, the two-story log house was completed in 1880. Four years later he began remodeling the mansion, adding a stone castle tower that included gargoyles carved with faces of himself, his wife, and his brother John, among others.

By 1880 Helen was pregnant with the couple's third child. Since the Dorseys had been devastated by the death of their daughter, Carlotta, in 1874, they were especially happy with the news of Helen's pregnancy. Because of Dorsey's secretarial role in the Republican National Committee and the upcoming presidential campaign, they decided Helen and young Clayton should return to her family's home in Oberlin for the arrival of the new baby. While the Dorseys were thrilled with the birth of baby Stephen in 1880, their happiness was short-lived. Like Carlotta, Stephen also died in early childhood.

Family tragedies continued for the Dorseys when Helen's brother and his wife later died in an accident. Although the Dorseys adopted the couple's son, George, the boy also died at an early age.

Along with the personal tragedies in his life, Dorsey became involved in yet another scandal during the 1880s. Four decades earlier Congress had established mail routes to remote places of the country, designated by "stars" on special route descriptions. With expansion to the West over the years, approximately ten thousand Star Routes were operational in the country by 1880.

The US Post Office Department operated the Star Routes

through independent contractors who placed bids for four-year contracts. By law the post office could only accept the proposal of the lowest bidder. But some groups of contractors put in bids from extremely low to exorbitantly high, manipulating the system so that low bids would drop out of the bidding and the high bidder would win the contract. Another fraudulent ploy was to win the low bid, then insist that customers were demanding more and faster services—which would increase costs by requiring additional horses, wagons, and delivery men.

By the late 1870s Congress had caught on to the schemes and launched an investigation into the Star Route contracting process. Names of high government officials and prominent senators were mentioned, including Arkansas senator Stephen W. Dorsey. Claims surfaced that the senator was sending out blank bonds and bids for his friends to sign. With no viable proof against Dorsey, however, the congressional committee took no action.

In February 1882 eight defendants were finally brought to trial for overfunding postal contracts. The two main offenders were Assistant Postmaster General Thomas J. Brady and ex-Senator Stephen W. Dorsey. Along with his partners in crime, Dorsey was accused of defrauding the government out of $412,000.

The defense's hefty financial resources supplied skillful lawyers, along with ample funds to bribe witnesses. The result was a hung jury. The jurors voted to convict Postmaster Brady by a vote of ten to two, and nine of the twelve jurors also voted to convict Dorsey. A new trial began in late 1882. Bribery of jurors was suspected but never proven conclusively. After nine months the jury returned a verdict of "not guilty as indicted." Though Dorsey was never convicted of a crime concerning the case, many individuals were convinced he was guilty.

The Star Route scandal and trials were reported by major newspapers across the country, including the *New York Times*. President Garfield, who had vowed to punish the individuals responsible for bilking the US Postal Service out of hundreds of thousands of dollars, did not hide his disdain of Dorsey, reportedly stating that the ex-senator "had a screw loose in his moral makeup." Expanding upon Garfield's remarks, the *Boston Herald* noted that "the star router never had enough moral make up for a screw to take hold of."

Though Dorsey was found not guilty, the Star Route scandal destroyed his reputation and political ambitions. But the resilient Stephen Dorsey shrugged off the ordeal and returned to New Mexico in search of another adventure.

Before long, Dorsey was regarded by many New Mexico residents as a member of the Santa Fe Ring, a group of wealthy landowners and lawyers who controlled all political and economic affairs in New Mexico Territory, as well as much of the real estate.

Seeking a base for a large cattle operation, Dorsey acquired ownership of six hundred thousand acres in New Mexico through the Una de Gato land grant in 1877. When the grant was exposed as fraudulent, he developed a new strategy to obtain the acreage and water to support his stock-raising activities. Under this new tactic he planned to gain control of water resources by acquiring properties under homestead and preemption laws. The objective of these laws was to provide parcels of western land to individual families who would reside on the properties and develop the acreage. Providing massive tracts of land for stock-raising activities was not the true intent of the laws.

Over the next few years, Dorsey enlisted the help of his employees and cowboys to acquire tracts of land, piece by piece, for his own financial gain. Each employee claimed a 160-acre parcel of public domain land under the homestead and preemption laws, then turned the property over to Dorsey. This ploy, along with the purchase of existing ranches, allowed Dorsey to gain control of water resources and grazing access on public land. Moreover, he still retained control of the original six hundred thousand acres previously acquired through the Una de Gato land grant. Though legal officials were convinced that the land grant was fraudulent, the property remained under Dorsey's control.

In June 1884 Inspector Frank D. Hobbs of the General Land

Office reported that he had investigated seven claims located near Dorsey's base of operation. One property had been conveyed to Dorsey, four to his neighbor, and two claims were jointly filed by Dorsey and his neighbor. In addition, Dorsey had fenced off land on the public domain that provided valuable water resources for his cattle operations. Worse yet, Colfax County deed books held claims filed by names that could not be readily identified, increasing suspicions that the names were fictitious. Hobbs came to the conclusion that "an honest investigation would result in the cancellation of hundreds of fraudulent entries, and many thousand acres of land would be thrown open to entry by actual settlers."

Three years later the *North American Review* published an essay, "Land-Stealing in New Mexico," that discussed Dorsey's unscrupulous deals. Referring to the Una de Gato grant, the article noted, "When the forgery of the grant was demonstrated in 1879, and he thought it unsafe to rely on that title, he determined to avail himself of the Homestead and Preemption laws." The author of the article, Surveyor General George Julian of the General Land Office, also stated, "Mr. Dorsey, who was already in possession of thousands of acres of the choicest lands in the tract, at once sent out squads of henchman, who availed themselves of the forms of the Pre-emption and Homestead laws, in acquiring pretended titles, which were conveyed to him, according to arrangements previously agreed upon."

Dorsey shot back at the charges with a rebuttal in the *North American Review's* October 1887 issue, pointing out that a farmer could not cultivate a waterless tract of 160 acres, the maximum allowed under the public land laws. He also claimed that the system of distributing western lands could not meet even the most minimal needs for raising cattle. As he pointed out, the government erred in "dealing with the arid region, largely which is, at its best, mere grazing land, as if it was of the same character, condition, and capacity as the purely agricultural domain of the country."

Dorsey's public response fell on deaf ears. By the time the federal investigation came to a close, he was indicted for fraudulent land claims. Although he was not convicted of any crimes, the controversy permanently scarred his reputation, which had been previously tarnished by the other scandals throughout his career.

By the early 1890s Dorsey had dispensed of portions of his New Mexico land holdings. During this time he was hit by numerous lawsuits, including some cases related to shares of the Arkansas Central Railway that he had sold back in the 1870s. Even his magnificent New Mexico mansion became tangled up in lawsuits from creditors.

In October 1892 Dorsey had nearly reached the point of destitution. In desperation he converted his mansion into a sanatorium for tuberculosis patients. When the venture proved unsuccessful, he moved to Denver, Colorado, and invested in irrigated farming and mining operations.

Back in New Mexico, creditors continued to hound Dorsey and place liens on his home, even though the identity of the actual owner of the property was unclear due to numerous legal battles. When Helen died in 1897, however, the courts determined that she was the legal owner. The mansion was sold at a public auction in 1901, and was purchased by one of the creditors.

Eventually Dorsey moved to Los Angeles, California, and married a woman by the name of Laura Bigelow. He died on March 20, 1916, and his body was transported to Fairmont Cemetery in Denver, Colorado, for burial beside his first wife, Helen.

Though Stephen Wallace Dorsey achieved success as a soldier, politician, and businessman throughout his lifetime, the majority of his accomplishments were overshadowed by controversy and scandal. Yet despite the numerous charges against him, Dorsey was never found guilty of a crime. One of his lasting legacies, however, is his election to the US Senate as a Republican from Arkansas. After Dorsey stepped down at the end of his term in 1879, another Arkansas Republican would not serve in the senate until Tim Hutchinson won the seat in 1999.

Cassie Chadwick

Con Artist
1857–1907

A fashionably dressed woman stood in the lobby of New York City's Holland House, an elegant Fifth Avenue hotel, and impatiently surveyed the massive room. Where was James Dillon?

It was the spring of 1902, and Cassie Chadwick had traveled to New York by train from her home in Cleveland, Ohio, as part of an elaborate scheme. Now she had to find James, a Cleveland attorney and a friend of her husband's, to set her plan into motion.

Within moments she had located James and was marveling at the delightful coincidence of bumping into him in New York. Cassie quickly explained that she was heading to her father's house to pick up some papers. Would James like to escort her there?

Without a moment's hesitation about helping his friend's wife, James hailed a carriage. Cassie gave a Fifth Avenue address to the driver. As soon as the carriage rolled to a stop in front of a four-story mansion belonging to steel magnate Andrew Carnegie, Cassie picked up her skirts and climbed down from the carriage with a promise to James that she would return within a few moments.

The butler opened the door to the mansion. Cassie politely asked for the head housekeeper, wishing she could see the look on James Dillon's face as he waited in the carriage and watched her step inside the Carnegie mansion.

With a pleasant smile that concealed her deceit, she told the housekeeper that she was checking the references of a maid who had once worked for the Carnegie household. The housekeeper insisted no one by that name had ever worked at the mansion.

Cassie Chadwick
THE CLEVELAND PRESS COLLECTION, MICHAEL SCHWARTZ LIBRARY,
CLEVELAND STATE UNIVERSITY

Apologizing for the error, Cassie adjusted the brim of her hat and bid farewell to the woman. Just as she turned to leave, she slipped an envelope out of her purse. As she climbed back in the carriage, an astonished James Dillon couldn't contain his curiosity. Was Andrew Carnegie truly her father?

At that instant the envelope slipped from Cassie's fingers. The contents spilled out of the envelope and conveniently landed in James's lap, just as she had planned. James stared down in disbelief at a pair of promissory notes for $250,000 and $500,000, signed by Andrew Carnegie, and securities valued at a total of $5 million.

Cassie pleaded with him not to reveal her secret to anyone. Yes, she was Andrew Carnegie's daughter, but her illegitimacy had caused a great deal of guilt for the steel baron. Out of a sense of responsibility, "Daddy" often presented her with large sums of money. She even anticipated inheriting millions from his estate upon his death.

Though James vowed never to reveal her secret, the shrewd Cassie Chadwick knew the attorney would never keep such a remarkable story to himself. And her instincts were correct. Cleveland's financial community was soon buzzing with whispers of her wealth and connection to the Carnegie name.

Cassie's theatrical demeanor easily masked her lies, so James Dillon never suspected that she was a complete stranger to Andrew Carnegie. But the successful Cleveland attorney was only one of many people duped by Cassie Chadwick. Pretending to receive millions of dollars in gifts from a wealthy millionaire was just one of her many sophisticated plots to keep her coffers full and running over. Moreover, the Carnegie sham allowed her to secure nearly $15 million in loans for nearly a decade.

But the cunning Cassie did not limit her deceitfulness solely to financial schemes. The four men who married Cassie were all fooled by her fraudulent ploys, and each of the marriages ended in disaster. Worse yet, Cassie Chadwick was only one of the aliases she had used over the years.

Cassie Chadwick was born as Elizabeth "Betty" Bigley on October 10, 1857, in Ontario, Canada. As the fifth of eight children, she grew up with her brothers and sisters on a small farm. But Betty had much bigger dreams than the rural community could hold. With hearing loss in one ear and a slight speech impediment, she was a quiet child who often sat in silence for hours. She declined to tell anyone about her most private thoughts. One of her sisters, Alice, later recalled that young Betty often lapsed into a trance-like state, so lost in her daydreams that she barely noticed her surroundings. Alice also remembered that Betty practiced writing signatures of family members, repeatedly penning the names until her versions were identical to the originals.

Betty plotted her first scheme at age thirteen, presenting a letter to a local bank that stated she had inherited some money from an uncle. The notice—forged by Betty—appeared so genuine that the bank supplied her with checks so she could access the funds in advance. When the funds never arrived at the bank, Betty was reprimanded and warned to never repeat the mistake again.

Undeterred by the failure of her first scam, Betty continued devising fraudulent strategies as a young adult. In 1879, at age twenty-two, she was arrested in Woodstock, Ontario, for forgery. In this instance she tried to pay for an item with a note that exceeded the purchase price and requested the difference in cash from the merchant. Though the note was proven to be fraudulent, Betty was acquitted on grounds of insanity.

Seeking a fresh start, Betty left home to live with her sister Alice and her husband in Cleveland, Ohio. But it wasn't long before Betty was scheming again, secretly attempting to use her sister's furnishings as collateral for a bank loan. Once Alice's husband discovered what Betty had done, he kicked her out of the house.

Betty moved to another neighborhood in Cleveland, where she wasted no time in meeting prominent individuals in the area. Dr. Wallace S. Springsteen was particularly captivated by the young woman with a slight lisp to her voice and a hypnotic gaze. Betty soon accepted his proposal of marriage.

Betty Bigley and Dr. Springsteen were married in a civil ceremony conducted by a justice of the peace in December 1883, as reported by the *Cleveland Plain Dealer*. But the couple did not live happily ever after. Apparently overjoyed that she had married a wealthy physician, the new bride went on an extravagant shopping spree. Within days numerous merchants showed up at the couple's home, demanding to be paid. Stunned and angry that his wife had taken advantage of him, and concerned with his dwindling bank account, Dr. Springsteen resentfully paid his wife's debts and promptly told her to leave. The marriage ended only twelve days after it had begun.

Betty packed her bags and left Cleveland, deciding to become a different person. Traveling from town to town and living in boardinghouses, she transformed herself into Madame Marie Rosa. As a charming clairvoyant she scammed merchants and conned new friends. In Erie, Pennsylvania, for instance, she faked a serious illness and complained that she lacked the funds to return home to Cleveland.

Local residents collected enough money to send her back to Ohio. When they later requested repayment of the funds, they were saddened to learn that poor Marie had died. In sharing the news of Marie's death with her Pennsylvania friends, Betty included a sweet tribute to the deceased that she'd written herself.

Although Betty's recorded movements during this period are sketchy, history shows that she married twice, exchanging vows with two clients of her clairvoyant services. After a brief marriage to a Trumbull County farmer named Scott that ended in divorce, she wed businessman C. L. Hoover. Although the couple had a son, Emil, Betty sent the boy to Canada to be raised by her parents and siblings.

In 1888 C. L. Hoover died. With fifty thousand dollars in hand from the proceeds of her late husband's estate, Betty moved to Toledo and assumed yet another identity. Setting up as a clairvoyant, she offered her services as Madame Lydia Devere. One client, Joseph Lamb, was especially enchanted by Madame Devere and paid ten thousand dollars for her services as his financial advisor. Like many victims who fell under her spell, Joseph claimed she had "eyes of almost hypnotic brilliancy," as well as hypnotic powers that could convince anyone to do anything she asked.

Joseph could not refuse the madame's request to cash a promissory note for her at his bank in Toledo. Of course, Madame Devere had forged the signature of a prominent Cleveland resident on the note, which was written for several thousand dollars. After Joseph cashed several more checks for her, totaling forty thousand dollars, the banks realized they were dealing with a pair of forgers. Both Betty and Joseph were arrested.

The jury rightfully believed that Joseph had been a pawn in the fraudulent schemes, and he was acquitted of all charges, but Betty was convicted of forgery and sentenced to ten years in the Ohio State Penitentiary. Staying in character as a clairvoyant behind bars, she predicted the warden would lose five thousand dollars in a business deal before dying of cancer. Both predictions came true. She also pleaded for the parole board to give her a second chance, writing countless letters that expressed regrets for her past actions and promises to change.

After Betty served three and a half years of her sentence, Ohio governor William McKinley—who would later be elected to the nation's highest office—signed the official papers for her release. Since prison officials required regular reports from parolees, Betty obediently complied by reporting from Canada during the first two years of her release. In 1895 she reported that she had returned to Cleveland, once again to reside with her sister Alice.

Betty returned to Cleveland with a new lease on life and another new identity. This time she chose the name of Cassie L. Hoover, assuming the last name of her late husband. Before long she made the acquaintance of a wealthy widower, Leroy S. Chadwick. A descendant of one of Cleveland's oldest families, Leroy was a respected physician in the community. Although history does not reveal the definite place or circumstances of their first meeting, some sources contend that the doctor visited a brothel that Cassie was operating. When he complained of rheumatism in his back, Cassie generously offered to relieve his pain with a massage, and Leroy fell in love with her "compassion." Other sources make no mention of a brothel and simply state that "a Mrs. Hoover advised him to try massage" to help ease his arthritic back pain.

Like many other men, Dr. Chadwick could not resist the charms of Cassie Hoover. The couple married in 1896, even though the doctor knew little to nothing about his bride's lurid past. Dr. Chadwick's friends, who also knew nothing about Cassie, were surprised the esteemed physician would marry someone out of their social circle.

The couple resided in the doctor's palatial residence on Euclid Avenue, Cleveland's most prestigious address, along with Dr. Chadwick's daughter from his first marriage. Cassie, now settled down for the first time in her life, brought her son back from Canada to permanently live with her and her new husband in Cleveland. For the next seven years, she stayed out of trouble and lived quietly among the city's wealthiest and most influential residents.

Even though she restrained herself from scamming anyone, Cassie could not resist spending her husband's money. She redecorated the doctor's mansion with fine furnishings with no regard to the cost, filled her jewelry chest with thousands of dollars' worth of diamonds, pearls, and precious jewels, and ordered custom clothing and hats from New York.

But Cassie regressed to her old ways in 1902 when she headed to New York and duped attorney James Dillon into believing that she was Andrew Carnegie's illegitimate daughter and heiress to the millionaire's estate. The deception set the stage for Cassie to accumulate thousands of dollars in fraudulent loans. When word spread through the Cleveland financial community that she was Carnegie's child and heir, bankers were happy to loan huge sums of money to Cassie. But the unsuspecting bankers had no clue that they were being duped by one of the state's greatest con artists of all time.

With money rolling into her coffers from her scams, Cassie spent freely and lavishly. She entertained friends at parties that cost thousands of dollars. She chartered private rail cars for trips, and she showered her friends with presents. One Christmas season, for instance, she purchased eight pianos as gifts for friends.

Cassie's scam centered around obtaining loans from large financial institutions like Ohio Citizen's Bank, Cleveland's Wade Park Banking Company, New York's Lincoln National Bank, and at least a dozen more. She would take out a loan at one institution and then use a second loan to repay the first one, with each loan being larger than the last. Bankers were so convinced that she was good for the loans that they would even lend money to Cassie from their personal accounts. For example, Cassie convinced Charles Beckwith, the president of Citizen's National Bank, to lend his private fortune to her, amounting to $120,000, along with an additional bank loan of $240,000.

Charles Beckwith was convinced that he was not assuming any unusual risks in dealing with the elegant Mrs. Chadwick because her assets were worth far more than any amount of money he could loan to her. "I have seen three chests full of jewels owned by Mrs. Chadwick," he later recalled. "There were diamonds worth a king's ransom. Her jewels alone must have been worth half a million dollars."

Bankers also loved that Cassie would agree to pay high rates of interest on loans without a second thought. Through the prestigious Euclid Avenue Baptist Church, Cassie connected with Herbert Newton, a Boston investment banker. He eagerly wrote a check to her from his business for $79,000 and an additional personal check for $25,000, for a total of $104,000. And he must have been extremely proud of himself when she signed a promissory note for more than $190,000 without questioning the exorbitant interest.

Cassie fooled a multitude of bankers until her scheme started to crumble in November 1904. After Cassie stalled numerous times on repaying her loans, Herbert Newton realized he had been duped. The physician's wife had no intention of repaying the loans, and Herbert knew he had no hope of recovering the principle, much less the interest.

Herbert filed a lawsuit against Cassie in Cleveland's federal court. To prevent Cassie from moving and hiding her money, the lawsuit stipulated that Wade Park Bank continue to hold the promissory notes that Cassie had presented at the bank from her "father," Andrew Carnegie.

At the same time, Charles Beckwith's bank encountered financial difficulties. Now suspicious of Cassie, he made several attempts to collect his money. Though she promised to settle her debts, the banker never received a dime from her. In late November the bank collapsed, and Charles was financially ruined. Reports surfaced that he collapsed when he learned that the Carnegie securities held by Wade Park Bank were worthless.

Cassie denied all charges in the lawsuit, claiming it was all a huge mistake and she fully intended to repay the money. Moreover, she repeatedly denied that she had ever claimed to be the illegitimate daughter of Andrew Carnegie.

In December 1904 enterprising reporters began probing into Cassie's past as they covered the sensational story. Rumors surfaced that she may have assumed the identity of Madame Lydia Devere during the early 1890s and served prison time for forgery. Within a few days two women who had worked at the Ohio State Penitentiary in Columbus positively identified Cassie as the person who had been imprisoned under the name of Lydia Devere.

Press coverage of the story made headlines across the globe. Dr. Chadwick, who was visiting Europe with his daughter when the news hit the newspapers, swiftly arranged to return to the United States. When his ship docked in New York, he was arrested on charges of being an accomplice to his wife's crimes. Though the charges were soon dropped for lack of evidence, the physician still paid a hefty price for being the husband of Cassie Chadwick. To pay off some of the creditors demanding repayment from Cassie's many loans, the doctor lost his beautiful home and all his savings.

Many experts think Cassie may have spent millions of dollars within a few years to support her lavish lifestyle. The total amount of her fraudulent dealings has never been calculated with absolute certainty. Some historians believe she scammed more than six hundred thousand dollars from her victims, but they also contend that many more individuals may have remained silent about their losses.

Decades of deception rapidly came to an end for Elizabeth "Betty" Bigley, also known as Madame Marie Rosa, Mrs. Wallace Springsteen, Madame Lydia Devere, Mrs. C. L. Hoover, Cassie L. Hoover, and Cassie L. Chadwick. Realizing she would soon be arrested, Cassie fled to New York and checked into a luxurious hotel. When Cleveland authorities tracked her down, she was arrested on numerous fraud charges and conspiracy to commit fraud.

In March 1905 she was found guilty of conspiracy to defraud a national bank and sentenced to ten years in the state penitentiary. Andrew Carnegie personally attended the trial and later examined the infamous promissory notes. He insisted the entire scandal could have been avoided if anyone had bothered to contact him. "I have not signed a note in the last thirty years," he claimed.

Charles Beckwith, the bank president, visited Cassie in jail, even though she was personally responsible for causing his bank to collapse and ruining his personal wealth. "You've ruined me," he said, "but I'm not so sure yet you are a fraud."

While imprisoned, in late September 1907, Cassie complained of severe stomach pains. The illness intensified, and she lapsed into a comatose state within a few days. The woman who had climbed to the highest pinnacle of American society by fraudulent schemes died alone in the Ohio State Penitentiary on October 10, 1907, her fiftieth birthday.

Alfred Knapp

Serial Strangler
1863–1904

On August 7, 1894, a young couple walked from their home along the Miami and Erie Canal, now known as Central Parkway, heading to the offices of the *Cincinnati Enquirer* in downtown Cincinnati. The husband, thirty-one-year-old Alfred Knapp, had spent more time looking for a job in recent months than actually working. In and out of prison for most of his adult life, Alfred now claimed he was looking for yet another job.

As he went inside the newspaper office to inquire about an advertisement for work, Jennie Knapp, Alfred's second wife, waited outside the building. She had been more than patient with Alfred. He had gone to prison three times during their nine-year marriage. While working odd jobs in Cincinnati, he served one sentence for stealing a pool table, another for stealing cash and jewelry. The last crime was far more serious, involving an attack on a woman in broad daylight. Found guilty of assault charges, he was sentenced to the Ohio State Penitentiary in Columbus and served his time from July 1890 to November 1893.

The following day Cincinnati police recovered the body of a young woman from the canal. Cuts and bruises appeared on her head, face, and neck. Police assumed that broken glass on the bottom of the canal had scratched the body, causing the abrasions. They also attributed her fractured skull as the result of a canal boat ramming into the body.

The body was soon identified as Jennie Knapp. Alfred told police they had gone to the newspaper office together on the previous day. Jennie had waited outside the building, he claimed, but

Alfred Knapp
OHIO HISTORY CONNECTION

by the time he left the office, she had vanished. He insisted he had nothing to do with her death.

During the coroner's investigation, Alfred's two sisters offered valuable information to officials. Mamie King testified that Jennie had visited her on the day before her death. Distraught and tearful, the young woman announced that she was pregnant. "What will I do? I have got nothing to take care of my baby with when it is born," she said. Mamie noted that Jennie was often sad and melancholy, but she assumed the depression stemmed from Alfred's long absences in prison and his lack of steady work. Mamie also recalled that Jennie once said that "for two pins" she would jump into the canal.

Mattie, Alfred's other sister, confirmed that Jennie had never wanted to be a mother and had threatened suicide in the past. Mattie suspected her sister-in-law was mentally unbalanced and believed she took her own life.

The testimonies convinced the coroner that Jennie Knapp had committed suicide by drowning. With the ruling a postmortem examination was deemed unnecessary, and the case was closed.

Alfred Knapp had escaped being a suspect in his wife's mysterious disappearance and death. But it was not the first time that someone in his life had met an untimely demise—nor would it be the last. In the end Alfred Knapp would become known as a serial strangler, responsible for the deaths of five young women.

The son of Cyrus and Susannah Knapp, Alfred Andrew Knapp was born in Indiana in 1863. At age eighteen Alfred went to prison for the first time. After serving a two-year sentence at the Joliet Prison in Illinois, he returned home to live with his parents and siblings in Terre Haute, Indiana. Within a short time he met sixteen-year-old Emma Stubbs, who lived next door to the Knapp family with her parents. After a hasty courtship Emma became the bride of Alfred Knapp.

But the marriage lasted only three months. Convicted of stealing jewelry, clothing, and cash, Alfred headed to prison again. In 1885 he was released from the correctional facility in

Jeffersonville, Indiana, and headed to Lawrenceburg. While living in the small town, he met a young woman by the name of Jennie Connors. Three days later the couple exchanged wedding vows.

During his marriage to Jennie, Alfred could not stay out of trouble. Between serving three prison sentences, he worked at odd jobs, including traveling with several circuses as a utility man and hustler. At one point Jennie also worked at one of the circuses as a cook. She hated the job, however, and suggested they move to Cincinnati, where Jennie's father worked as a streetcar conductor.

Living with his wife in an apartment building in downtown Cincinnati after his release from prison in November 1893, Alfred continued to have trouble finding decent work. But as he aimlessly walked the streets of Cincinnati in the summer of 1894, he committed three violent crimes. His first victim was a little girl, Emma Littleman. On June 21, 1894, he choked Emma to death and hid her tiny body under boards at a lumberyard near Gest Street. Police later recovered the remains of the little girl, but were baffled by the identity of her murderer.

Six weeks later a heated argument erupted between Alfred and a former girlfriend, Mary Eckhart. Fearful she would tell his wife that he had been seeing another woman, Hannah Goddard, Alfred strangled Mary to death with a towel in a house on Walnut Street on August 1. Police ruled that the victim's death was a suicide. Six days later police also determined that the death of Jennie Knapp was a suicide by drowning.

Within six weeks of Jennie's death, Alfred married Hannah Goddard. The newlyweds moved from place to place in Cincinnati, struggling to earn a living. After residing in Hamilton, Ohio, for a brief time, they landed in West Indianapolis in the summer of 1895. Alfred wasted no time getting in trouble. Within days of moving to the city, he was arrested for assaulting a young girl. Years later he confessed to murdering Ada Gebhart in Indianapolis in July 1895, although he was never charged with the crime. Alfred was convicted of the assault on the young girl, however, and was sent to prison for the sixth time, sentenced to serve ten years at the Indiana State Prison in Michigan City.

Furious about the conviction, Alfred swore vengeance on everyone from the sheriff and prosecutors to the judge and jury. After serving seven years of his ten-year sentence, he was released on parole in June 1902. Within days mysterious fires erupted at barns that belonged to the sheriff and one of the jurors in Alfred's trial. Though both men blamed Alfred for the destructive blazes, they could not find any solid proof of his guilt.

While Alfred served time in the Indiana prison, Hannah lived with her sister-in-law, Mamie King, and her husband, Edward, in the northern Cincinnati suburb of Cumminsville. Upon Alfred's release from prison in June 1902, the couple rented an apartment in Hamilton, Ohio.

By early fall Alfred was on the prowl again, searching for another unsuspecting person to become his latest victim. On the evening of September 16, 1902, Alfred approached two little girls as they peered into the front windows of Koerber's grocery store. Promising to give candy to the girls, he lured the children into a nearby alley. Alfred worked quickly, first attacking four-year-old Hattie Motzer by knocking her unconscious with a blunt instrument. Then he lunged for Hattie's sister, Stella. Grabbing the neck of the six-year-old, he stabbed her head with a "knife that she saw in the moonlight," reported the *Daily Republican-News*, Hamilton's local newspaper.

Streams of blood poured down Stella's face, and the child screamed so loudly that Alfred released his hold on her and darted out of sight. The little girl ran home, leaving a trail of blood behind her. The gory path led her family back to the alley, where little Hattie lay unconscious. Though Hattie was seriously wounded, she eventually recovered from the brutal assault.

Within hours of the attack, little Stella Motzer blamed Joseph Roth for the assault. A familiar face to the Motzer family, Joseph regularly sold homegrown vegetables in the alley from a horse-drawn cart. In the early morning hours after the attack, the police arrested Joseph at his home. The man vehemently denied the charges.

Fred Koerber, owner of the grocery store, believed that police had arrested the wrong person. The man outside his store on the night of the attack was not Joseph Roth. The grocer, who personally knew Joseph, claimed the attacker was a stranger. Moreover, veteran Hamilton policemen insisted that bloodhounds did not sniff their way from the scene of the crime to the Roth house, as had been previously reported. Newspapers also printed interviews with other Hamilton cops who were convinced of Joseph Roth's innocence. Though mounting evidence showed that the state was prosecuting the wrong man, a trial date was set for March 1903 in Butler County Common Pleas Court. County prosecutor Warren Gard, a future US congressman, was named to prosecute the case for the state.

Meanwhile, Alfred Knapp was busy plotting the murder of his third wife, Hannah. A few days before Christmas in 1902, Alfred told several people that his wife had left town to visit a sick relative and had never returned. He also told a different version of the story to some women who purchased two of his wife's hats and several dresses, stating that Hannah had left him. After selling his furniture and other household belongings to neighbors, Alfred handed over seventy-five dollars in back rent to his landlord. Then he headed to Indianapolis, Indiana.

As weeks passed without any sign of Hannah, Alfred's brother-in-law, Edward King, suspected that Hannah would not leave town without informing anyone of her plans. With the aid of a detective, Edward discovered that Alfred had rented a horse and buggy and loaded it with some belongings shortly before Christmas. He also learned that Alfred's parents, who had recently relocated to Cincinnati from Indianapolis, had just received a letter from their son. The letter, postmarked in Indianapolis, revealed that Alfred married Anna May Gamble on February 3. The Knapps were familiar with Anna May, a neighbor who lived with her foster father on the same street as the Knapps when they had resided in Indianapolis.

Although Hamilton investigators had no proof that Alfred had murdered Hannah Knapp, they were highly suspicious of the man who had taken a new wife while the previous one was still missing. Even if Hannah had walked out on her unscrupulous husband, no divorce records had been located. Figuring they could nab Alfred on bigamy charges, two Hamilton police officers set off for Indianapolis.

The officers quickly located Alfred, who was living in a dingy cellar apartment in Indianapolis with his fourth wife, Anna May. Brought into the Indianapolis police station for questioning, Alfred again claimed that Hannah had left town a few days before Christmas to visit a sick family member and had never returned. When police informed Alfred they intended to arrest him for bigamy and transport him back to Hamilton, Alfred shrugged. "Well, if they want to prove bigamy on me, they'll have to find Hannah," he said flatly. After the officer assured the convicted felon that they could find the young woman, Alfred mumbled, "I guess you won't find her."

The next morning officers escorted Alfred Knapp back to Hamilton, Ohio, by train and booked him into the county jail. Surprisingly, Alfred signed a written confession on February 26, 1903, and admitted killing five young women by strangulation. He conceded that he had killed three females in Cincinnati during 1894: Mary Eckhart, young Emma Littleman, and his second wife, Jennie. He also confessed to killing Ada Gebhart in Indianapolis in 1895, and his fifth and final victim, his third wife, Hannah, in Hamilton, Ohio, on December 22, 1902. One week after his confession, Hannah Knapp's naked, decomposing corpse was discovered floating in the Ohio River near New Albany, Indiana.

Alfred filled in the missing details of each crime for reporters and the police. Less than a week after killing Mary Eckhart, Alfred revealed that he had argued with Jennie while walking along the Miami and Erie Canal in downtown Cincinnati. "I sat her down on the bridge and choked her to death," he told reporters, then tossed her lifeless body into the canal.

He also explained the demise of Hannah Knapp. He murdered his third wife at home on a cold December day and placed her lifeless body into a wooden box. After renting a horse and wagon, he hauled the box to the Great Miami River south of town. Within moments he removed the container with Hannah's body from the wagon and plunged it into the frigid water.

As he revealed the horrible specifics of his grisly crimes, Alfred almost seemed to revel in the methods of his madness. "I always kill from behind," he told the *Cincinnati Times-Star*. "I get them in front of me. Then, I clutch them by the throat, placing my knee on the back and bend them over. They struggle, but not long. They look into my face, but I don't mind that. . . . Some kind of a desire to kill took hold of me, and I could not resist the temptation."

On the opposite end of the scale of emotions, Alfred broke down in tears when Emma Littleman's father confronted him in his jail cell. As Herman Littleman later revealed to a *Times-Star* reporter, Alfred apologized to the dead girl's father, saying, "I am as sorry that the child is dead as you are."

Shortly before the opening of Joseph Roth's trial in early March, Alfred claimed from his jail cell that he could help the man accused of attacking the two young sisters. Hearing the claim, Joseph's attorney subpoenaed Alfred Knapp to testify at the trial. When Alfred took the stand, the defense attorney tried to persuade him to admit he had been at the location of the crime on that September evening, but Alfred claimed he had been visiting a local doctor.

The prosecuting attorney, Warren Gard, also put young Stella Motzer on the stand. After being forced to display her scalp wound, she cried so hysterically that the judge ordered to delay the proceedings.

Still, the defense attorney prevailed during the five-day trial. By putting Alfred Knapp on the stand, he had planted seeds of doubt about Joseph Roth's guilt in the jurors' minds. Moreover, strong character witnesses had defended the local street vendor, and the prosecution's timeline that placed Joseph at the scene of the crime had been totally derailed.

After deliberating for just twenty minutes, the jury acquitted Joseph Roth of all charges. By then both the public and the press were convinced that Alfred Knapp was the only person capable of attacking two innocent little girls. Since his arrest and confession, national and local newspapers had compared "Knapp the Strangler" to London's "Jack the Ripper." With the acquittal of Joseph Roth, one local newspaper wasted no time in speculating on the true identity of the attacker: "The verdict meets with the general endorsement of public opinion and there are many who think that despite his denial, it was Alfred Knapp in reality who committed the crime. It was the dastardly work of some fiendish degenerate and he seems to fill the bill."

In spite of Alfred's confessions, his family stood behind him throughout the ordeal, insisting he could not be mentally responsible for his crimes. According to one newspaper report, Cyrus Knapp, Alfred's father, "died of a broken heart" after his son's arrest and incarceration.

In July 1903 Alfred Knapp went on trial for the murder of Hannah Knapp in Butler County Common Pleas Court. Despite Alfred's insanity plea, he was found guilty of the charges and sentenced to death by electrocution.

The Ohio Supreme Court upheld the verdict on appeal. Alfred's defense attorney claimed, "The decision is a great surprise to me. It completely upsets all my notions and calculations about law."

Alfred also expressed surprise that the supreme court refused to grant a new trial, but he remained defiant with the press. "I will never go to the electric chair," he declared to a *Times-Star* reporter. "It is not my fate; [I] still have friends in Cincinnati who will now come to the front and save me." Despite Alfred's prediction, no one could stop the electrocution of the man who had heartlessly strangled five innocent women. In the final moments of his life, Alfred tried to make light of his impending doom by grabbing an accordion and playing a lively

version of the popular song, "A Hot Time in the Old Town Tonight."
On a more serious note, he also penned one last confession:

> *To Whom It May Concern:*
> *Joe Roth is innocent of the attack on the Motzer children*
> *on September 16, 1902. I done that myself, but there was no*
> *intention of committing rape on them. Now, I am doing this*
> *to clear Joe Roth's name. I assaulted them myself.*
> *Alfred Knapp*

On August 19, 1904, Alfred Knapp was strapped into the electric chair at the Ohio State Penitentiary in Columbus and shocked with more than seventeen hundred volts of electricity that killed the prisoner within minutes. The prison warden declared that the execution was "the most successful I ever had." After the electrocution Dr. H. H. Hoppe, a Cincinnati neurologist, examined the prisoner's brain and declared that nothing could be found that would indicate insanity. In his opinion Alfred Knapp had been perfectly sane.

The next morning the Columbus funeral home handling the interment of Alfred Knapp opened its doors at six o'clock. More than three thousand curiosity seekers filed into the building to view the infamous strangler "calmly reposing in a handsome casket of black cloth with silver handles," the *Republican-News* reported. The Cincinnati chapter of the Daughters of America, in honor of Susannah Knapp, Alfred's mother and a member of the chapter, provided a spray of flowers and white carnations to adorn the serial strangler's casket. He was buried in Mount Calvary Cemetery in Columbus, Ohio.

Dr. James Howard Snook

Gold Medal Murderer
1879–1930

On a pleasant summer morning in 1929, a pair of teenage boys stomped through knee-high weeds at the New York Central Railroad rifle range in Columbus, Ohio. With rifles in hand the teens were eager to try shooting their weapons for the first time at the popular rifle range. It was Friday, June 14, only the second day of summer vacation for the boys, who both attended North High School in Columbus.

They had taken only a few steps across the field when they noticed a farmer plowing a two-acre patch of land with a two-horse team about two hundred yards away. Deciding to warn the farmer that they would be shooting in the area, the boys headed in the man's direction. But as they tromped through the weeds, they suddenly noticed a swarm of flies buzzing in front of them. They took a few more steps, and then stopped cold.

The dead body of a woman was lying on her left side in the field. The teens could not see the woman's face, but they could tell she had brown hair and was wearing a bloodstained, brown crepe dress with a white collar.

Little did they realize that their gruesome discovery would initiate the most celebrated case of murder in the capital city's history.

The boys called out to the farmer, who agreed to watch over the body while the teens went to the police. Within the hour they returned to the shooting range with two police officers. The coroner and a crime scene photographer from the Ohio Bureau of Investigation arrived a short time later.

Dr. James Howard Snook

When the men turned over the body, they saw the woman's throat had been slit with a sharp knife. She had sustained multiple blows to the face and skull. They also noticed the woman was wearing a man's wristwatch. The crystal had fallen out, and the hands were stopped at 9:58—possibly the time of the crime on the previous evening.

The men grimly transported the body to the city morgue. Since no purse or other identification was found with the victim, officials had a "Jane Doe" on their hands. Who was this young woman? And why would anyone want to murder her in such a brutal, barbaric way?

About the same time as the discovery of the victim, sisters Alice and Beatrice Bustin were wondering why their roommate, Theora Hix, had not returned home on the previous evening. The three women shared a small flat above the State Drug and Supply Company, about a block away from the Ohio State campus.

By late Friday afternoon Alice Bustin knew something was terribly wrong, and she called the police to report that Theora was missing. She described the missing roommate as a brunette who always wore a man's watch—her father's watch—on her right wrist. As soon as police heard the description, they suggested that Alice and her sister go to the morgue.

By 5:30 p.m. Alice and Beatrice Bustin had arrived at the mortuary and positively identified the battered corpse as Theora Kathleen Hix, a second-year Ohio State medical student two months shy of her twenty-fifth birthday. Police also obtained a photograph of the victim, a casual sorority photo showing a fresh-skinned, moderately attractive young woman with short brown hair and a sly smile.

The sisters told police that they were not overly concerned when Theora did not come home for the night. They assumed that she had spent the night at the home of a local couple who frequently employed her to stay with their two young daughters when they were out of town. But shortly before noon on Friday morning—about a half hour after the body had been found at the rifle range—the sisters became alarmed. A friend of Theora's from the university called, concerned that Theora had not shown up for a luncheon appointment.

Alice, also a second-year student in the medical college, told police that Theora was a good student who loved to read. Beatrice, a technician in the medical laboratory at the university, said Theora chatted freely about insignificant matters, but stayed silent about her personal life. The sisters suspected she had been spending time with someone because she was rarely home in the evenings. They also revealed that Marion Meyers, a horticulture professor at the university, had been an acquaintance of Theora's, but they did not know anything about the extent of the relationship.

Though Theora always seemed to have plenty of money, she planned to work part-time on the switchboard at the hospital over the summer. In fact, the last time the Bustins had seen Theora on the night of the murder, she was heading to Ohio State University Hospital to train on the switchboard for her summer job as a relief operator.

Columbus police would eventually learn that Theora was the only child of a couple who had been married for twenty years before becoming parents. Her father, Dr. Melvin T. Hix, was an instructor of medicine in Bradenton, Florida. Born on Long Island, New York, she attended New York City public schools and graduated from a college preparatory school in Massachusetts, Northfield Seminary, in 1922. Her father later told the *Columbus Dispatch* that he and his wife sent her to Northfield Seminary because they wanted the very best moral and religious influence for their daughter. Theora graduated from Ohio State University in 1927 and had enrolled in the medical college after receiving her undergraduate degree.

Police launched the investigation to unravel the mystery of her killer's identity and find an explanation for her brutal death. They quickly learned that on the evening of the murder, Theora sat with Bertha Dillon, a switchboard operator at the Ohio State University Hospital, for an hour or so to learn the layout of switchboard.

Shortly after 7:30 p.m. Theora announced she had to leave for a date, but promised to return between 9:00 and 9:30 p.m. But, as Bertha explained, Theora never came back to the hospital.

Next, investigators talked to a taxicab driver who had picked up a woman matching Theora's description at about the same time Theora departed from the hospital. The driver claimed the woman seemed edgy, requesting to be driven through town so she could find a man in a Ford coupe. After nearly an hour of searching without success, she told the driver to take her back to the OSU campus.

Neighbors who lived near Theora's apartment building provided even more information to police, revealing they had seen the college coed in recent months with a balding, middle-aged man who wore horn-rimmed glasses and drove a new, dark blue Ford coupe.

The next morning, the *Ohio State Journal* printed a description of the wanted man. "Somewhere in Columbus there is a man who is heavily built, wears horn-rimmed glasses, is about forty, and drives a Ford coupe," the article stated. "This man holds the secret of the murder of Theora Hix. This man, name unknown, has been seen frequently with the murdered girl. If you know of such a man, you may hasten the solution of one of the most gruesome crimes in the history of Columbus by informing police of your knowledge or suspicions."

Meanwhile, investigators attempted to locate Marion T. Meyers, a thirty-five-year-old horticulture expert from the agriculture department at Ohio State University. Although they did not find him at home, a close friend of the college professor told detectives that Marion knew the identity of the man who owned a blue coupe and had been a constant companion of the murdered girl in recent months. The man was Dr. James Howard Snook, a professor of veterinary medicine at the college.

Investigators were stunned by the revelation. Dr. James Snook was not only a highly respected professor and veterinarian, but also a well-known, world-class marksman who had won two gold medals at the 1920 Olympics. He shared a lovely home in Columbus with his wife and daughter and frequently attended the Methodist church with his family. How could such a respectable and accomplished gentleman be connected to such a horrendous crime?

His background revealed nothing to indicate he was capable of murder. James Howard Snook was born on September 17, 1879, in South Lebanon, Ohio, a rural community about thirty miles northeast of Cincinnati. He was the only son of Albert and Mary Keever Snook. His sister, Bertha, was six years his junior.

As a teen at South Lebanon High School, James was described as a polite, studious, and quiet student who loved to practice target shooting. His father, Albert, had a lifelong interest in racehorses and constructed a racetrack on the family's two-hundred-acre farm. Growing up surrounded by animals and horses on the farm sparked James's interest in veterinary medicine.

After earning a two-year commercial business degree at Nelson's Business College in Cincinnati, James returned to the farm for three years before entering Ohio State University in 1905. He earned his doctorate in veterinary medicine three years later. He was a member of the Veterinary Medical Society and Sigma Phi Epsilon, and helped found the veterinary fraternity, Alpha Psi.

As a student at Ohio State, James became interested in handguns. By 1911 he had established a world's record with the revolver. A year later he won five matches with "remarkable scores" at the national championships, competed successfully in international matches, and clearly established himself as one of the nation's premier shooters. As an undergraduate at Ohio State, he also became associated with the Military Aeronautics School on campus, where he taught rifle and small-arms shooting to US Army recruits during World War I.

On January 1, 1910, he secured a position as a teaching assistant in the College of Veterinary Medicine at Ohio State and gradually moved up to assistant professor. He achieved the status of full professor in 1921. While teaching at the college, he invented a surgical instrument for the spaying of female cats and dogs that became widely known as the Snook hook. Veterinarians still use the device today.

Throughout his teaching career, James Snook continued to refine his shooting skills. In qualifying trials for the 1920 Olympics at Quantico, Virginia, he was selected as an alternate for the pistol-shooting team. When one of the five team members could not make the Olympic competition, James became an official part of the team and headed to Beverloo, Belgium, outside Antwerp.

James excelled in team competition. The US group beat both Greece and Switzerland in the team competition for the military pistol at thirty meters to win the gold medal. In the team match for free pistol firing at fifty meters, the team again took the gold, this time over Sweden and Brazil.

Returning home with two gold medals, James turned his attentions to romance. He and Helen Thatcher Marple of nearby Newark, Ohio, were married on September 11, 1922, at the King Avenue Methodist Church in Columbus. A graduate of Ohio State University with a degree in education, Helen had been a sixth grade teacher before her marriage. Their only child, Mary "Jill" Snook, was born in 1927.

Despite the sterling reputation of James Howard Snook, the professor matched the physical description of Theora's most recent companion. Moreover, he had recently purchased a blue Ford coupe. On Saturday morning, June 15, two days after the murder, Columbus investigators picked up James and brought him to police headquarters. At the same time, detective Otto Phillips brought Marion Meyers to the police station. Both James and Marion were arrested and held for questioning.

During Marion's interrogation, investigators learned he had been more than just a friend to Theora Hix. In fact, he and the co-ed had been intimate on several occasions. Though Marion had proposed marriage to Theora, she had laughed and rejected the idea. He also revealed that Theora had been seeing Dr. James Snook for some time. On Thursday evening, the night of the murder, Marion said he had talked briefly with a friend at about nine o'clock and then retired for the evening. His friend later backed up Marion's claim.

Throughout several hours of questioning, Marion repeatedly insisted that he had not laid eyes on Theora in fifteen days. Realizing he could be a prime suspect in the murder, he could not contain his nervousness. In sharp contrast to Marion's edgy behavior, however, James Howard Snook remained calm and collected.

During questioning, Dr. Snook presented a feasible alibi for the night of the murder. Early in the evening he went to his office to work on an article for *Hunter-Trader-Trapper*, a popular monthly magazine. James had served as the publication's gun and ammunitions editor for more than a decade. After leaving the office he mailed some letters and visited a pharmacy not far from the university. He then picked up an evening paper and returned home for the evening.

But he did not deny that he knew Theora Hix. With little coaxing he freely told investigators that he had known Theora since June 1926, meeting her when she began working as a stenographer for the veterinary school. He also stated that he had financed a portion of her college expenses for some time, but was no longer doing so. Throughout the questioning detectives noticed that Snook remained calm, didn't contradict himself, and appeared to tell the truth.

Investigators learned more details about the relationship between James and Theora after a woman arrived at the county jail on Saturday evening. Mrs. M. M. Smalley explained that she ran an apartment house on Hubbard Avenue. A man had rented a room from her several months ago, she explained, and he looked like the picture of Dr. Snook that had appeared in the newspapers. Moreover, the woman who had claimed to be his wife resembled the newspaper photograph of Theora Hix.

Investigators escorted Dr. Snook from his cell to the jail office. "Good evening, Mr. Snook," the woman said as he entered the room.

He made no attempt to hide his acquaintance with the woman. "Good evening, Mrs. Smalley," the professor answered with a smile.

Both parties told their stories to detectives, obviously making no effort to withhold information. On February 11, 1929, James rented a single, furnished room from Mrs. Smalley. He informed her that he and his wife would occupy the dwelling from time to time when they came to town for their employer, a salt manufacturer. The doctor signed the register, "Howard Snook and wife." Using his middle name and omitting any reference to doctor, he made little effort to conceal his true identity. In later stays at the apartment by "Howard Snook and wife," Mrs. Smalley met a young woman who claimed to be Mrs. Snook. The woman was the same female identified in newspaper photos as Theora Hix.

The day after the murder, James arrived at the apartment between two and three o'clock in the afternoon and informed Mrs. Smalley that he and his wife would no longer need the room. After paying the landlady, he left two keys behind—one belonging to him and a second key used by his "wife."

With this new information, investigators grilled James throughout the night and into the early morning hours. They informed him that police had found a bloodstained glove and cap during a search of his car. Since James was a veterinarian, the glove might have been used in an animal operation, and the stains on the cap might have come from the glove. But the items had been turned over to a chemist, who had verified that the source of the stains was human blood.

The interrogators found it difficult to break the professor's rigid demeanor until they mentioned a pair of soiled trousers that he had taken to the dry cleaners on Friday, June 14. When they revealed that tests confirmed the trousers held bloodstains, Dr. James Howard Snook crumbled. After weeping for nearly an hour, he wrote and signed a confession to the murder of Theora Hix. He also told investigators they could find the murder weapons—a knife and a hammer—in a toolbox in the basement of his home. Detectives quickly retrieved the items, complete with bloodstains.

Marion Meyers was quickly released from jail. With a signed confession and two murder weapons as evidence, Columbus police knew they had solved the mysterious case.

The trial of Dr. James Howard Snook commenced on July 24, 1929. Three tables were set up across one end of the courtroom to accommodate forty members of the press, including "star" reporters of the day who wrote for national newspaper syndicates.

For the next two weeks, the jury of eleven men and one woman heard the case. Theora was described by friends and college professors as a studious, athletic girl, highly regarded by her associates. Jurors learned that neither Theora's roommates nor her parents were aware she had a boyfriend.

The most dramatic moment of the trial was the testimony of the defendant. Taking the stand, James admitted that he and Theora drove to the rifle range on the evening of the murder for the sole purpose of having sex in the parked car. But as soon as he mentioned that he planned to take his wife and daughter to his mother's house for the weekend, Theora became enraged. The co-ed damned his family and threatened to kill them "to get them out of the way."

James paused in his testimony, removed his glasses, and wiped tears from his eyes. He then dropped the biggest bombshell of the trial, explicitly describing how Theora opened his trousers and performed oral sex on him. He claimed she inflicted such unbearable pain on him that he "very nearly twisted her arm off" to make her stop.

"Damn you!" Theora screamed. "I will kill you, too."

The prosecuting attorney asked James why he had not previously mentioned the sexual encounter to anyone before taking the stand. "Simply because I was ashamed of it, ashamed of any sex perversion because I never knew anyone that would do that before," he answered.

James then continued with his testimony. After threatening to kill him, Theora grabbed her purse and slid out of the car. Fearing she would shoot him with a small pistol that he had previously given to her, James said he hit her with the ball of a hammer. After he delivered a second blow, "she slid right down on the ground, and I followed her out," he testified. "I got up behind her and I hit her once more with the hammer and she went down and her head hit against the running board of the machine, and that is all I can remember of hitting her." He claimed that by hitting her four or five times with a hammer he had "stunned" her, but he did not kill her. He also insisted that he did not remember slitting her throat with a knife, although he did recall tossing her purse out the window of his car on the drive home.

James's testimony was so shocking that respectable newspapers would not print it. However, an enterprising court stenographer hastily assembled a printed booklet with all the sordid details that was soon available on the street corners of Columbus.

The jury began deliberating the case shortly before four o'clock in the afternoon of August 14, 1929. After praying they would pass the right judgment, the twelve jurors discussed the case for a brief time. Only eighteen minutes later, they returned to the jury box. The foreman announced that they had found Dr. James Snook guilty of murder in the first degree.

On the evening of February 28, 1930, James Howard Snook was put to death in the electric chair. After a pre-dawn ceremony conducted the next morning by the minister of King Avenue Methodist Church, the body was buried in Green Lawn Cemetery. Once hailed as a gold medal champion, Dr. James Snook would be forever known as a gold medal murderer in the annals of Columbus history.

Eva Brickel Kaber

Murderer for Hire
1881–1931

On the evening of Friday, July 18, 1919, a frantic male voice broke through the silence of a luxurious home in Cleveland, Ohio. "Murder!" the man screamed. "Utterback, come quick! Murder!"

The cry for help came from the second-floor bedroom of Daniel F. Kaber, owner of the elegant residence on fashionable Lake Avenue. At age forty-six the once-healthy man had been confined to bed for months, paralyzed from an unknown illness. Now, around 10:30 p.m., he was calling out to his male nurse, F. W. Utterback, who was sleeping in a bedroom on the third floor of the house.

Though Utterback was in his sixties, he ran down the stairs in his bare feet with the speed of a much younger man. He charged into Kaber's bedroom, and then stopped cold at the sight in front of him. Kaber was lying on the floor in a pool of his own blood. A bloody knife was nearby.

The nurse dropped to his knees beside his patient and asked what had happened. Kaber, groaning in pain, spoke in broken sentences. "A man with a cap. Look for a man with a finger almost bitten off; I bit his finger. I think there were two of them. My wife had this done!"

At that moment three other occupants of the home appeared at the door of the room: Kaber's stepdaughter, Marion, accompanied by a girlfriend who was sleeping overnight at the house, and Kaber's mother-in-law, Mary Brickel. The trio of women immediately began screaming at the sight of the bloody scene.

Authorities were quickly notified, and Dan Kaber was rushed to Lakewood Hospital. Doctors discovered he had been stabbed

The Lake Avenue home of Daniel and Eva Kaber
THE CLEVELAND PRESS COLLECTION, MICHAEL SCHWARTZ LIBRARY, CLEVELAND STATE UNIVERSITY

twenty-four times. Kaber had five abdominal wounds, six buttock wounds, eleven stab wounds to the scrotum, and numerous facial and throat scratches. Though physicians worked hard to save his life, Dan Kaber did not survive, dying shortly after one o'clock on the following afternoon. Two phrases that he constantly repeated during his last few hours on earth were "a man with a cap" and "wife had this done."

Eva Kaber, Dan's wife, had not been home on the evening of the murder. In fact, about one week before the crime, she had announced to her family that she planned to visit her sister, Mrs. H. J. McGinnis, for a few days. Eva left Cleveland on Wednesday, July 16, two days before the murder, and headed to her sister's home in Cedar Point, Ohio.

She returned to her home at about five-thirty on the afternoon of her husband's death, appearing stunned when she learned of Dan's murder. She also seemed surprised to discover silverware scattered across her dining room floor, indicating that an apparent robbery had been interrupted. Known for her audacious, pragmatic personality, Eva stayed true to character and wasted no time grieving over her loss. She quickly posted a reward for her husband's killers, arranged Dan's funeral, and filed his will for probate.

When Cuyahoga County coroner P. J. Byrne launched the investigation into Dan Kaber's murder on the morning of July 23, Eva was called into the police stationing for questioning. With a valid alibi that placed her about sixty miles away from Cleveland on the night of the fatal attack, she appeared to be an unlikely suspect. Still, she had been the caretaker of an invalid husband with substantial financial assets, and investigators suspected she had strong motives for wanting her husband dead. Eva denied any involvement in the murder, but she wavered between stony calmness and tearful outbursts throughout the interview with prosecutors. She also suggested the murder must have been the result of a botched robbery instead of a crime directly targeted at her husband. "I can't imagine who could be guilty of such a deed. I never heard that my husband had enemies," she said.

The other occupants of the plush Lake Avenue residence were also questioned by police. Marion McArdle, Eva's daughter by her first marriage, occupied the bedroom next to her stepfather's. At age nineteen Marion was a typical teen who loved music, her friends, and having a good time. Though she was attending Smith College, her main goal in life was to establish a career as a chorus girl. A neighborhood friend, Anna Baehr, was spending the night with Marion on the evening of the murder. After catching a movie at a local theater, the pair had retired for the night behind closed doors in Marion's room.

With some prodding from investigators, both girls admitted that Dan's screams had awakened them around ten-thirty on Friday evening. "There was no one call for help, but many screams," Marion finally admitted. "It will be a long time before we forget those screams!"

Mary Brickel, Marion's sixty-seven-year-old grandmother, told detectives she carefully locked the doors and windows on the first floor before going to bed that evening. Like her granddaughter, Mary admitted that the sounds of her son-in-law's screams had jolted her out of a sound sleep around ten-thirty that evening.

Police reluctantly released all four women, unable to legally hold them at the police station any longer. Still, the investigation continued. Within a few weeks an autopsy revealed that Dan's corpse contained nearly forty grains of arsenic. But police could not trace the source of the arsenic, and they could not prove who had administered the poison to Dan Kaber.

Despite the prosecution's suspicions about Eva's guilt, the case was eventually closed for lack of evidence. Eva submitted claims to collect the proceeds on her husband's insurance policies, sold their neocolonial home, and left town as a wealthy widow.

At age thirty-nine Eva Catherine Brickel Kaber had not always lived a luxurious lifestyle. She came from a humble background, born into a large family of eight children. By 1919 four of her siblings were dead, and one of her brothers, Charles, had been sentenced to prison for theft.

As a young schoolgirl, Eva possessed a violent, uncontrollable temper. She often threw fits of rage and even physically attacked her schoolmates when she failed to get her own way. A known troublemaker, she frequently ran away from home. At age sixteen she was caught stealing eighty-five dollars from a friend and landed in an alternative school, the Home of the Good Shepherd, for a brief time.

The following year Eva obtained employment as a chambermaid for the wealthy residents of a mansion on the east side of Cleveland. Always superstitious, she was a frequent customer of fortune-tellers and mediums. So the seventeen-year-old must have been delighted when a medium informed her that she would always get what she wanted in life. Unbeknownst to the teen, the medium recorded observations about her clients in handwritten notes. Eva Brickel, she noted, was "bold and confident, but not very smart."

During this time Eva met and married a barkeeper, Thomas McArdle. Though the marriage lasted only two months, Eva walked away from her groom with a lasting memory of their union: a pregnancy that would later result in the birth of her only daughter, Marion, in 1900. But the young mother left her child in the care of her parents as she pursued single life once again. Eva soon married for a second time, to David Frinkle, a local barber. This marriage also ended after only a few months.

Since Eva had learned to manipulate people to get what she wanted, she may have schemed and plotted to win the heart of the son of a wealthy Cleveland printer, Dan Kaber. Whatever her methods she succeeded in luring him into a hasty marriage in September 1907. But Dan's Jewish father, Moses Kaber, did not approve of the union. The elder Kaber was particularly disturbed by the thought of his son being united in marriage to a gentile.

Dan Kaber may not have known many details about his wife's previous marriages. But in more than a decade of living with Eva, he most likely discovered that she was domineering and demanding. And during the last six months of his life, he may have suspected that she was trying to kill him.

In November 1918, eight months before his death, Dan became violently ill with a suspected case of influenza. His physical health steadily declined and even worsened in the following weeks. After exploratory surgery for possible cancer that was never confirmed, his physicians could not diagnose the cause of his misery. Near the time of his murder, he had lost the use of his limbs and was basically confined to his bed.

To an outsider Eva Kaber must have appeared to be the perfect wife, attentive to her invalid husband and insistent that she personally feed him. But several foods that she prepared for him—particularly soups and strawberries—caused the poor man to get even sicker. He tried to complain to his father and brother about the odd taste of paprika in his food, but confiding in his family was impossible with Eva's constant presence in his room.

But one person, Dan's seventy-one-year-old father, was certain of Eva's guilt. From the beginning Moses Kaber never doubted that his daughter-in-law was responsible for Dan's death. And he vowed that his son's killer would be brought to justice—no matter the cost. Since the police had closed the case, Moses took matters into his own hands and contacted the Pinkerton National Detective Agency, the most famous private investigators in the world.

Within weeks Pinkerton detectives were on Eva's trail, following her as she traveled from town to town. But the detective agency also found Ethel Berman, one of Eva's Lakewood friends, who was more than willing to help pin the death of Dan Kaber on his widow.

Ethel had known Eva for more than a decade. Though she did not approve of Eva's catty, heartless personality, she maintained a friendship with her after Dan's murder. On the day after the funeral, Ethel had been particularly distressed that Eva was actually laughing about the clothes she had selected for her husband's burial attire. "To think that I laid him out in a dirty shirt," Eva said with a wicked laugh. "Dan wasn't worth a clean shirt!"

Though Ethel was happily married with a young son, she could not refuse the Pinkertons' offer to work as an agent on the Kaber case. She later explained that she left her home for several months for the sake of justice, believing she could gather evidence to convict her friend of first-degree murder.

The Pinkerton Agency tracked down Eva in New York City, where Ethel was getting a crash course in detective work at the agency. Ethel managed to reach out to her friend on the pretense that she was a bitter wife who could no longer tolerate her husband—much like Eva herself. The two women were soon traveling together, attending movies, and eating at fine restaurants.

Ethel swiftly realized that her traveling companion was a very troubled woman who spent large sums of money seeking advice from fortune-tellers and mediums. She also talked obsessively about her late husband's death. One evening Eva cried out in her sleep, "I did it! I did it! I did it!" When Ethel asked her about the statements, Eva immediately lashed out at her friend, demanding to know if she was working for the Pinkerton people. Ethel swore she was not associated with Pinkerton or any other detective agency. "I swear to God that I hope to go home and see my son blind before I am in with the Pinkerton people," she vowed.

Still, Eva became increasingly suspicious of Ethel, and the women soon parted ways. Ethel returned to Cleveland, where she immediately befriended Eva's mother, Mary Brickel. Ethel had known Mary for years, and she had always hated the way Eva treated her mother. For years Eva forced her mother to do all the household laundry without any compensation for the work. Meanwhile, Eva insisted that Dan give her four dollars each week to pay the "laundress."

Ethel forged a friendship with the older woman, and the two often shopped, dined, and watched movies together. One day, as the pair settled into their seats at a movie theater, Mary finally spilled some concrete information on the case. Two movie patrons seated directly behind the two women distinctly heard every word. Not so coincidentally, the strangers were Pinkerton detectives. "She did it and she did it for money," Mary said, adding, "If they try to put it on Charlie, I'll tell all I know!" Charlie—Mary's favorite son and Eva's brother—was a likely suspect, considering his history of run-ins with the law.

Along with Mary's statement, Ethel located another piece of valuable evidence during one of her many visits to the Kaber household: a letter from Eva. Addressed to Marion the letter revealed that Eva did not have enough money to pay her husband's killers for their work.

Finally, with some valid evidence in hand, Lakewood police called Mary Brickel and her son, Charles, into police headquarters for questioning on May 31, 1921. Hoping to trap the grandmother into talking, the prosecutor nodded toward Charles and told the jailer, "Lock this man up and charge him with the murder of Dan Kaber! He's the one who did it!"

Unwilling for her son to take the rap, Mary revealed the details of Dan's murder to investigators. On June 1, 1921, first-degree-murder indictments were issued against Eva Kaber, Mary Brickel, and Marion McArdle.

Eva was arrested in New York City on Saturday, June 4. Marion, who was traveling across the country as a member of the chorus line in *Pretty Baby*, was picked up two days later. Both women were brought back to Cleveland and locked up behind bars.

During the investigation the Pinkertons learned that Eva Kaber had been a regular customer of clairvoyants and mediums for years. Within days of Eva's arrest, Cleveland police also arrested Erminia Colavito, a fortune-teller and potion vendor, in Sandusky, Ohio. They also picked up a thug from Cleveland's Little Italy, Salvatore Cala, suspecting he was one of two men who had been commissioned by Eva to murder her husband. They also identified a second suspect, Vittorio Pisselli, who had already fled the country for Italy.

During June 1921 all the pieces of the puzzle surrounding Dan Kaber's murder fell into place for investigators. First, they learned Dan had been reluctant to pay his stepdaughter's tuition at Smith College in the fall of 1918, which infuriated his wife. Eva also suspected Dan was contemplating changes to his will.

Furious with her husband, Eva consulted a Cleveland medium, Erminia Colavito. Telling the medium about Dan's selfishness, she begged for a "potion" to set him straight. Though Erminia later insisted the potion was only olive oil and ginger ale, the mixture also contained arsenic, which would bring about Dan's mysterious symptoms and physical decline, starting with his bout of "influenza" in November 1918.

By late June or early July 1919, Eva paid another visit to the medium. Frustrated that the potion had not yet worked its magic on her husband, she told Erminia that she needed a quicker solution to her problem—and would pay any amount to have her husband killed.

The medium swiftly referred her client to two young Italian men. By early July the plan was set. Eva would leave town and arrange for her mother to let the two men into the house in the middle of the night. Valuable items would be scattered across the home to appear as if a burglary had been interrupted while the men crept up the stairs to murder Dan Kaber in his bed. Eva promised to pay between three and five thousand dollars for the deadly deed.

Back at home Eva recruited her mother and daughter to help with the scheme. On the evening of July 15, Salvatore and Vittorio arrived at the Kaber residence to run through each step of their scheme in preparation for the actual murder. Marion's school friend, who was also present in the house, later told police that Marion suddenly began playing the piano, obviously to drown out the conversation between Eva and the two strange men.

On July 16 Eva drove to Cedar Point to establish her alibi. On the evening of July 18, the killers entered the house through a door left conveniently unlocked by Mary Brickel. In the darkness they made their way up the stairs and into Dan Kaber's bedroom. Salvatore Cala held down the paralyzed invalid—and got badly bitten on his thumb—while Venturino Pisselli repeatedly stabbed the helpless man. Salvatore later testified that the helpless cripple cried out, "Mercy! Mercy! What have I done to you?"

Within minutes their task was done, and the two men fled the house and jumped onto a streetcar bound for the east side of town. Later, Marion's girlfriend recalled that her hostess held her back from dashing into the stepfather's bedroom when they first heard his screams for help.

By the time Eva's trial opened on June 28, 1921, both Marion McArdle and Mary Brickel had signed confessions implicating Eva for the murder. Moreover, Eva had confessed to most of the facts of the conspiracy murder plot against her husband. Though the state was demanding death by the electric chair, William J. Corrigan,

Eva's court-appointed lawyer, hoped to save his client from death with a plea of insanity. The brilliant defense attorney would later rise to fame at the first trial of Cleveland's Sam Sheppard, a young doctor charged with murdering his beautiful wife.

The proceedings in the county courthouse attracted throngs of curious spectators, fueled by front page headlines of the conspiracy. To the great disappointment of press and public, Eva never took the stand, but her dramatic behavior supported the insanity argument. As psychiatrists and family members testified about her instability and crazy behavior, she became visibly upset. She collapsed more than once during the trial and had to be removed from the courtroom.

On July 16, 1921, after a short period of deliberation, the jury returned to the courtroom. Limp and on the verge of collapse, Eva was escorted into the room by two deputies. The jury foreman quickly announced a verdict of guilty for first-degree murder with a recommendation of mercy, meaning Eva would face life in prison rather than death in the electric chair. With the reading of the verdict, Eva became the second woman in Cuyahoga County to be convicted of first-degree murder.

"I'll be out in a year. I'll be free!" she bragged to reporters as she departed for the Ohio Reformatory for Women in Marysville.

Incarcerated at the Marysville reformatory, Eva eventually settled down to prison life. She worked quietly in the prison sewing room until prison officials intercepted a letter written by Eva to Marion. Offered fifty thousand dollars for the film rights to her life story, Eva planned to use the money for an escape. She would bribe prison authorities with some of the money, Eva revealed to her daughter, but if the head matron and her husband could not be bribed, she would arrange to have them murdered. Once prison officials read about the scheme, Eva was placed in solitary confinement.

By the late 1920s Eva's health began to fail. Although she underwent successful goiter surgery, she refused treatment for a gastric tumor in 1927. Most likely Eva hoped to win parole for medical reasons, but the tumor progressed before she could convince officials of her worthiness for parole. Bedridden for the last few months of her life, she died on April 12, 1931, at age fifty. Ironically, her death came just as the governor of Ohio was considering her latest parole request. Lung complications, heart disease, and a stomach tumor were listed on Eva's death certificate as the causes of her demise. Marion, who was beside her mother at the time of her death, arranged for Eva to be cremated in Portsmouth, Ohio.

Some participants in the conspiracy to murder Dan Kaber escaped punishment for the crime. Marion McArdle was found innocent in a subsequent trial, acquitted on the grounds that she was intimidated by her mother into cooperating with the scheme. Grandmother Mary Brickel was not charged, due to her cooperation with the prosecution and insufficient evidence for her role in the murder. Erminia Colavito was acquitted at her own trial, despite evidence that her "potions" had successfully helped several women in getting rid of their husbands. Both Salvatore Cala and Vittorio Pisselli received life terms. Vittorio had been caught in Italy by detectives hired by Moses Kaber. A five-hundred dollar bill and Dan's Masonic ring were the only payments they had received from Eva for the murder.

With the deadly elements of murder, money, and mediums, the Kaber case remains one of the most infamous stories in the history of Cleveland, Ohio—and the only homicide that indicted a grandmother, mother, and granddaughter for first-degree murder.

Martha Wise

The Poison Widow of Hardscrabble
1884-1971

The small farming community of Hardscrabble, Ohio, offered very few social activities for residents to enjoy at the start of the twentieth century. Located in Medina County's Liverpool Township, Hardscrabble was situated more than twenty miles away from the big city of Cleveland. Left to devise their own amusements, the town's citizens centered their social lives around holiday celebrations and the rituals of church services, particularly special events like weddings and funerals.

By 1924 one Hardscrabble resident had attended so many funerals that she had earned the title of the "funeral hobbyist." Townspeople claimed that Martha Wise, a forty-year-old native of Hardscrabble, had attended every funeral within twenty miles of the town for two decades.

Martha's neighbors had much more to say about the unattractive, odd woman with a reputation for having a "cluttered brain." Most of the people who knew Martha Wise, however, would have never dreamed that she was capable of committing serial murders by poisoning multiple members of her own family.

Born in 1884, Martha Hasel was the daughter of farmers Wilhelm and Sophie Gienke Hasel. During childhood she suffered from spinal meningitis and seizures that may have been caused by undiagnosed epilepsy. Slow and sickly, she was labeled as "mentally retarded, queer, and erratic" by her teacher, who also claimed she "could not learn." Like many farm girls of the time, young Martha received little formal education. She left school at age fourteen after completing the fifth grade.

Martha Wise

Along with having a difficult and unhappy childhood, Martha also experienced a host of imaginary ailments. She frequently visited the town's doctor complaining of problems that the physician could not verify. On one visit, for instance, she complained of a sore arm. The doctor quickly realized that the bruises on her forearm were actually leftover dyes that had been used to tint Easter eggs. On another visit with the same complaint, the doctor discovered that the blisters on her arm had been caused by rubbing turpentine into her flesh.

Lacking an education and marketable skills, Martha worked as a kitchen girl in various Medina County homes for several years. At times she ventured out to social events, like the "box social" she attended in 1906. During a box social, men bid on boxes of food prepared by the women in attendance. The winning bidder of a box not only won the food, but the chance to share the meal with the woman who prepared it. At this particular box social, Martha prepared a box of chicken sandwiches that received a winning bid from Albert Wise, a local farmer about twenty years older than Martha.

Soon Albert was courting Martha, and a marriage proposal and a wedding quickly followed. Though Martha may have hoped that marriage would improve her life, her hopes were shattered as soon as she moved to her new husband's one-hundred-acre farm. By all indications love had not been the primary reason that Albert had married her. Instead he had wanted an additional laborer to toil in the fields. The cruel groom forced his bride to plow the fields and slop the hogs like a common farmhand. If she refused, a beating would follow. The hard physical labor continued even after Martha became pregnant. The couple's baby, Albert, died soon after birth.

In the following years Martha gave birth to three more sons, Lester, Everett, and Kenneth, and a daughter, Gertrude. But her workload on the farm continued as usual, along with the responsibilities of raising four children. To escape the daily grind of the farm, Martha found the perfect excuse for getting away from the drudgery by attending funerals. Neighbors insisted that she never missed a chance to mourn the passing of a neighbor or an acquaintance, and some claimed she even attended funerals of complete strangers.

With Albert's sudden death, reportedly from an infected arm, Martha became a widow in late 1923. After she attended her own husband's funeral, Martha's emotional instabilities intensified. Her eldest son, Lester, later reported that she often roamed aimlessly through the countryside after dark, wandering through the fields as if she were searching for something or someone.

Martha admitted to her family that she was being haunted by visits from angels and white doves. Moreover, several neighbors claimed they saw her foaming at the mouth, rolling her eyes, and even barking like a dog. Most likely the behavior was caused by epileptic seizures that were never properly diagnosed.

At age forty with four children, a homely appearance, and known emotional instabilities, Martha Wise could hardly be considered a prime prospect for marriage. But within a year of Albert's death, Martha suddenly announced to her family that a man named Walter Johns had asked for her hand in marriage.

Sophie Hasel, Martha's seventy-two-year-old mother, and her uncle, Fred Gienke, strongly opposed the marriage. Both forbade her from marrying Walter, and Sophie even threatened to not only disinherit Martha, but also publicly disown her.

After a heated exchange of words, Martha conceded to her mother's wishes. She even agreed to come to Thanksgiving dinner at Sophie's home, a double dwelling that she shared with her son and Martha's brother, Fred Hasel. The festive Thanksgiving celebration, however, did not go smoothly. After eating dinner, several family members complained of mild stomach pain. A few weeks later Sophie's illness intensified. After several days of agonizing abdominal pains and leg weakness, she died on December 13, 1924. Her official cause of death was "influenza and inflammation of the stomach."

Martha sobbed uncontrollably at her mother's funeral and could not be comforted. Two days after Sophie's funeral, the family gathered at the Hasel house once again to mourn their loss together. Their moments of grief, however, were cut short as another wave of illness swept through the family. Martha's brother, Fred Hasel, along with his wife, son, and two other Hasel relatives, became sick after drinking coffee and water. Fortunately, every family member recovered within a few days.

On January 1, 1925, the family reconvened at the home of Fred Gienke, Martha's uncle, to celebrate the start of a new year. Within twenty minutes of eating pork stew and drinking coffee and water, eight family members were experiencing acute abdominal pains: Uncle Fred Gienke, his wife, Lillian, and six of their children, ranging from ages nine to twenty-five. Martha also complained of a mild bellyache. Oddly enough, her four children were not affected by the sudden illness affecting the rest of the family.

Lillian Gienke's pains became so severe that hospitalization was necessary. Doctors suspected that the cause of the sudden illness striking the family was ptomaine poisoning. But the attending physician noticed that Lillian's health problems—severe stomach pains and stiffening of the leg muscles—were also symptoms of poisoning from heavy metals. Since other family members were recovering, however, local health officials did not suspect foul play. "The family is highly respected in their community," officials stated. "There are no known enemies. There was no domestic trouble. No one is under suspicion." Still, Lillian Gienke died on January 4, 1925, only three days after entering the hospital.

As the family prepared to bury its second loved one within a month, a series of unexplainable fires erupted in Hardscrabble. At least ten barns burned to the ground, incinerating trapped livestock. Since the flames usually started at night while farmers and their families were safe in their beds, human lives were spared. Then Hardscrabble residents noticed that valuable items were missing from their homes, particularly jewelry and farm implements. The fires and thefts set the little community on edge. Was an arsonist and thief among them?

While the mysterious blazes continued, another wave of illness rolled through the Gienke family. On January 16, Fred Gienke Sr., his four children, and sister-in-law, Rose, experienced the same symptoms that had taken the lives of Sophie and Lillian. A Cleveland nurse, Rose Kohli, also became ill after making coffee at the Gienke house, although she soon recovered.

By the start of February, Fred and two of his children had been admitted to a local hospital for treatment. Unfortunately, Fred died in the hospital on February 8. The cause of death was listed as "inflammation of the stomach."

Once again doctors at the hospital suspected something amiss with the staggering number of illnesses and deaths in the same family, and they requested testing for the two Gienke children who remained in the hospital, Rudolph and Marie. This time local health officials agreed with the request. And the results confirmed the doctors' suspicions. The tests revealed large quantities of arsenic in the children.

Medina County authorities immediately launched an investigation into the deaths of Sophie Hasel and Fred and Lillian Gienke, as well as the illnesses of other family members. Their search soon led them to a local druggist, W. H. Weber. Pharmacy records revealed that Martha had purchased two ounces of arsenic at the Medina drugstore on November 24, 1924, and had signed for the purchase in the poison register, as required by law. The druggist revealed that Martha claimed she needed the poison to kill rats on the farm. Several days later she returned to the pharmacy and purchased another ounce of arsenic.

On March 1, 1925, Martha left Hardscrabble and traveled to Cleveland's Fairview Park Hospital to receive treatment for an arm infection. During the days she stayed in Cleveland for medical care, investigators realized that the recent chaos in their community—the fires, the thefts, and the poisonings—had abruptly ceased. Could Martha Wise be responsible for all the deaths and destruction?

Though the media did not know about local authorities' suspicions of Martha, the news of the murders and illnesses spread like wildfire. Numerous articles in Cleveland's three newspapers reported on the mystery and listed the names of the victims, including Martha, who had reported feeling ill after the New Year Day's meal at the Gienke home. The press also speculated on possible theories for the deaths and poisonings. Could the arsenic have originated in chemicals used on Hardscrabble apple trees? Were the illnesses caused by leaks in a gas stove in the Gienke kitchen?

In mid-March suspicions about Martha intensified when the *Cleveland Press* published an interview with Richard Gienke, one of the sons of Fred and Lillian Gienke. Richard claimed that Martha Wise had "threatened to get us. . . . After mother and dad died, we began to wonder about the poison, but didn't think of the threats. But when the rest of us kept getting sick, we remembered them."

With this new information in hand, local authorities decided to determine the true cause of Lillian Gienke's death. On Wednesday, March 18, Lillian's body was exhumed from its grave in the Myrtle Hill Cemetery. The county coroner, two physicians, and a chemist conducted a postmortem evaluation, and the report of their findings was disturbing. Lillian's stomach and intestines were saturated with enough arsenic to kill three people.

The Medina County sheriff, Fred Roshon, immediately left for Fairview Park Hospital in Cleveland. Finding Martha in the hospital's waiting room, he promptly placed her under arrest and announced he was taking her back to Medina County for questioning.

Sheriff Roshon escorted Martha into the prosecutor's office for an official interrogation. Waiting for her arrival were the coroner, a stenographer, and the sheriff's wife, Ethel Roshon. The group questioned Martha for two hours, but she repeatedly denied inflicting harm to her relatives.

The course of the investigation took a dramatic turn when a steady rain began to pound upon the windows, prompting the sheriff's wife to speak. "Listen to that rain," urged Ethel Roshon. "Do you know what it is saying, Martha? It is saying, 'You did it, you did it.' It is the voice of God, telling you to tell the truth."

It took only a few moments of listening to the raindrops before Martha broke down. "Oh, God, yes, I did it," she admitted. "The devil told me to."

In Martha's official confession, she said she purchased the first batch of arsenic in late November, telling the druggist she planned to "pound it into meat and put it into the cellar to catch rats." Instead she put "just a pinch" in her mother's water bucket on Thanksgiving Day, and continued poisoning the water until Sophie was dead. The second round of killings began on New Year's Day when Martha started to place arsenic in the Gienkes' water bucket. All in all, she poisoned seventeen people.

Moreover, Martha admitted that she set fire to ten houses and barns in recent months. "Some of the fires I started at night. Some of them I started in the daytime after the devil had told me at night to do it," she confessed. "I never stayed at the fires. . . . I slipped away to a hiding place and watched them blaze and crackle and burn." She also admitted stealing numerous pieces of jewelry from her relatives and neighbors.

The news of Martha Wise's confessions hit the papers with full force. One newspaper headline, "Brain monster warps souls of Medina killer," appeared on March 19, 1925, the day after the confession. Another newspaper declared the murders were a result of Martha's "craze for funerals."

Martha even elaborated on her motivations for the crimes to a *Cleveland Press* reporter, stating, "The Devil made me do it. He came to me in my kitchen when I baked my bread and he said, 'Do it!' He came to me when I walked the fields in the cold days and nights and said, 'Do it!' Everywhere I turned I saw him grinning and pointing and talking. I couldn't eat. I couldn't sleep. I could only talk and listen to the devil. Then I did it!"

Influenced by intense media coverage, the public demanded a murder trial. Though Martha's attorneys tried to make a case for insanity, psychiatric examinations convinced physicians that she was fit to stand trial. Medical experts concluded she was "of an inferior constitution and mental grade, but she is not insane."

Martha Wise went on trial for the murder of Lillian Gienke at nine o'clock on the morning of May 4, 1925, at the Medina County Courthouse. Hundreds of spectators arrived early for the chance to find seats. By the time the trial started, nearly two hundred people were packed into the courtroom and dozens more were standing outside.

Three of the Gienke children, crippled by consuming the arsenic, were brought into the courtroom to testify. One of the children had to be transported by stretcher, while the other two limped to their seats. But it was the testimony of Martha's oldest child, Lester, age fourteen, that proved to be highly damaging to his mother's case. Lester testified that he had overheard Martha talking about poison with one of her male friends. To make matters worse, he claimed his mother had warned her four children to never drink from the water buckets at the Gienke house.

The trial lasted ten days. Fifty-two witnesses took the stand, all characterizing Martha as eccentric, odd, and mentally incapacitated. Martha did not testify on her own behalf. The jury of seven women and five men deliberated for about an hour, then returned to the courtroom and announced a verdict of guilty for first-degree murder. They recommended mercy, which meant a life sentence.

As soon as Martha heard the verdict, she shifted her blame for the murder from the devil to her boyfriend. It was Walter Johns, she insisted, who had convinced her to murder her family. Walter denied everything, claiming he had no romantic interest in the crazy widow and actually felt sorry for her. Though police arrested him, they could find no evidence to support Martha's claims. In fact, they discovered that Walter was a dependable, steady worker at a Cleveland firm with five children of his own. After a few days of questioning, police released Walter for lack of evidence.

With a life sentence in prison inevitable for Martha, authorities arranged for her four children to be placed in adoptive homes. Though many thought Martha's mental state would rapidly deteriorate behind bars, she surprised everyone by adapting quickly to prison life at the Ohio Reformatory for Women in Marysville. Her prison assignments included working in the laundry and taking care of the chickens and ducks on the prison grounds.

Still, Martha remained haunted by hallucinations for years in prison. As she told one reporter in 1930, "I see ghosts. Every night they come and sit on the edge of my bed in their grave clothes. They point their fingers at me."

In spite of her good behavior in prison, officials denied Martha's request for parole three times: in 1946, 1951, and 1956. But her luck changed in 1962 when Ohio governor Michael DiSalle commuted her first-degree murder conviction to a second-degree charge, making her eligible for parole.

After serving nearly thirty-eight years in prison, Martha was released from the Ohio Reformatory for Women on February 2, 1963. Since all of her children declined to accept responsibility for their seventy-nine-year-old mother, and even refused to allow her into their own homes, the state arranged for Martha to live at a private nursing home in Blanchester, Ohio. As soon as Martha and her parole officer arrived at the nursing home, however, the operator of the facility had a change of heart and refused to admit Martha. The woman claimed the people of the small town of Blanchester would no longer conduct business with the nursing home if it harbored a criminal as violent as Martha Wise.

With no place for Martha to go, the parole officer took Martha to her own home in Cincinnati to spend the night. The following day Martha returned to the Ohio Reformatory for Women in Marysville to spend the remainder of her life behind bars. She died at the prison on June 28, 1971, at the age of eighty-seven, and was buried in Marysville.

Charles Arthur "Pretty Boy" Floyd

Public Enemy Number One
1904–1934

On Monday afternoon, October 22, 1934, Ellen Conkle answered a knock at the door of her farmhouse in Sprucevale, Ohio, and was surprised to find a stranger standing in front of her. A long-time resident of the rural community, the widow knew almost everyone in the area, and strangers were few and far between.

Beneath his disheveled appearance, the stranger appeared to be a young, attractive man about thirty years old. He quickly explained that he had gotten lost while hunting in the area and had spent the previous night wandering through the woods.

The man seemed polite and respectful. Since his dirty, unkempt looks justified his reasons for appearing on her doorstep, Ellen ushered him into the house and offered to prepare a meal for him. Since her husband's death, she had had few opportunities to fix a meal for a hungry man, and she quickly headed to the kitchen. Before long the man was rapidly consuming a large plate of spare-ribs, potatoes, and rice pudding. As he finished off the meal with a slice of pumpkin pie, he deemed the feast was "fit for a king" and offered payment of one dollar for the widow's trouble.

After eating, the man politely asked Ellen if she might have any recent newspapers that he could read. She handed over several editions of the local paper. The man stepped out to the porch, newspapers in hand, while she headed back into the kitchen. Before long the man returned and asked for her help in getting to Youngstown, Ohio. Ellen indicated that her brother and sister-in-law, Stewart and Florence Dyke, could possibly give him a ride

Charles Arthur "Pretty Boy" Floyd
COURTESY, LIBRARY OF CONGRESS, LC-USZ62-I34475

after they finished their work in the fields. Their car, she explained, was parked behind the corn crib.

The stranger thanked Ellen for her hospitality and went outside to wait in the front seat of her brother's Model A Ford. When the man explained he needed a ride to Youngstown or the nearest bus line, Stewart Dyke promised to take him part of the way. Just as they started to pull out of the farmyard, two cars came speeding down Sprucevale Road toward the Conkle farm. The stranger suddenly demanded that Stewart get the car behind the corncrib again. But as police and federal agents continued to approach the car, the man bolted out of the vehicle, holding a Colt automatic in his right hand.

Nine officers armed with pistols, rifles, and shotguns blasted away as the man dashed across the adjacent cornfield, heading in the direction of the woods with the agility of a seasoned athlete. Ninety-three shots were fired in his direction, but the man did not return fire. One bullet knocked him to his knees, but he got back on his feet and continued the race.

Within seconds another bullet knocked the man down. The lawmen rushed across the field and came to a stop beside him. "I'm done for," the man muttered. "You've hit me twice." The officials removed the gun from his right hand, which was paralyzed from a bullet wound, and found another gun tucked into the top of his trousers.

"Are you Pretty Boy Floyd?" one lawman demanded.

"I'm Floyd," the man said gruffly.

The same lawman asked what the wounded man could tell him about the Kansas City massacre, a recent gun battle that had resulted in the death of four law enforcement officers.

Floyd snapped, "I won't tell you anything, you son-of-a-bitch."

Those were the last words reportedly spoken by Charles Arthur "Pretty Boy" Floyd, known throughout the country as "Public Enemy Number One." Three patrolmen from East Liverpool carried the wounded man across the field and placed him at the base of a large apple tree, where he took his last breath. Within a few moments his body was propped up in the rear seat of a patrol car, sandwiched between two officers, and driven to the Sturgis Funeral Home in East Liverpool.

Floyd's mother sent a telegram from her home in Oklahoma, requesting no photography and no public display of her son's body. But it was too late. Her son's corpse was already on display on a gurney, and the public was filing into the funeral home to view the body. According to news reports, an estimated ten thousand people viewed the corpse that evening and on the following day. Numerous photos were snapped, and a pottery worker formed a facial death cast to make plaster masks for the officers who had tracked him down.

The capture and death of Pretty Boy Floyd made headlines across the nation, and newspaper articles recounted the tale of how one of the Depression era's most famous desperadoes was gunned down by local lawmen and federal agents. One Cleveland reporter even penned a whimsical poem, writing "Pretty Boy Floyd was a doggone fool / when he went to buy a dinner near East Liverpool."

In the excitement of reporting the story, a few reports contained inaccurate information. An extra edition of the *East Liverpool Review*, for instance, reported that a dozen bullet wounds had penetrated Floyd's body. Examiners later revealed only two bullet wounds could be found: one in the lower torso and another in the right forearm.

On the morning of October 24, Floyd's body was shipped home to Oklahoma on a Pennsylvania Railroad baggage car. Four days later his funeral and burial in Akins, Oklahoma, attracted more than fifty thousand people to the largest funeral in the state's history.

Long before his demise in Columbiana County, Ohio, Floyd had risen through the criminal world, killing at least ten people and robbing numerous banks along the way. The outlaw was well known to law enforcement officers throughout the nation, and he paid the ultimate price for his crime sprees in a cornfield at the Conkle's Ohio farm.

Few signs of criminal behavior were evident in Charles Arthur Floyd as a young boy, who was born on a farm in Bartow County, Georgia, near the town of Adairsville, on February 3, 1904. He was the second son and fourth child of Walter Lee and Mamie Helena Echols Floyd, who eventually expanded their family to eight children. From the beginning he was called "Charley" by everyone in the family.

Even though northwest Georgia had been the Floyd family's home for generations, Charley's parents decided to leave the area in hopes of finding more opportunities to provide for their family in the West. In 1911 Walter and Mamie chose to relocate to Oklahoma and live closer to several Floyd family members and friends who had already moved to the area from Georgia. The Floyds settled in Hanson, situated in Sequoyah County in far eastern Oklahoma near the Arkansas border, and eventually moved to Akin, Oklahoma.

Throughout the community Charley was considered to be a good boy who was always polite and truthful. Still, as a curious nine-year-old with a penchant for sweets, he couldn't resist stealing a box of cookies at the local grocery store. Since it was the first time Charley had been caught stealing, the store owner "tried to scare him up and show him he couldn't steal" and let the child go.

With little interest in schoolwork, Charley left school after completing the sixth grade. At fourteen he worked as a harvest hand in the Kansas and Oklahoma fields. Stocky and muscular with an athletic build, he soon discovered he loved a good fight. At a pool hall in Sallisaw, Oklahoma—his favorite hangout—Charley continually got into fights with rough oil workers.

With his good looks and pleasant personality, Charley was a magnet for young girls, and a sixteen-year-old farm girl from Bixby captured his heart. On June 28, 1924, he married Ruby Leonard Hargraves, whose dark eyes and hair reflected her Cherokee heritage. The newlyweds soon moved into a two-room wooden cabin on a farm near Akins. Their only son, Charles "Jackie" Dempsey Floyd, was born on December 29, 1924, and named in honor of the boxer Jack Dempsey.

By the following summer Charley was already weary of trying to provide for his family by farming. After trading five gallons of moonshine whiskey for a pistol, he announced to a neighbor, "I'm tired of tryin' to make a livin' with this stuff. Now I'm gonna give this here [gun] a try."

Charley packed his bags and joined a harvest crew traveling the midwestern states. He soon teamed up with another harvest worker and hoodlum, Fred Hilderbrand, for a crime spree in the St. Louis area. After robbing several Kroger stores, they set their sights on a much larger payout: the payroll at the headquarters of Kroger Food Stores. On Friday, September 11, 1925, the pair sat inside a stolen car and watched quietly as an armored car pulled up to company headquarters. As soon as a worker transported the payroll to a second-floor office, the young men made their move by bursting into the paymaster's office with guns drawn. They quickly confiscated the payroll, worth nearly twelve thousand dollars in cash.

The men fled the office and jumped into their stolen car. Gunning the engine, they led their pursuers on a wild car chase and managed to escape. Most likely Charley's nickname of "Pretty Boy" was the result of a newspaper interview with the paymaster. "The fellow who carried the gun was a mere boy—a pretty boy with apple cheeks."

Two days later Charley and his partner in crime were picked up by police in Sallisaw, Oklahoma. Within a few more days, they were formally charged with robbery. Charley was sentenced to five years in the Missouri State Penitentiary. He entered the prison to serve his term on December 18, 1925.

In January 1929 Ruby Floyd filed for a divorce in the Tulsa court system, charging her imprisoned husband with neglect. Charley did not contest the divorce, and Ruby maintained custody of their son.

By the time Charley was released from prison on March 7, 1929, four years behind bars had made him a hardened man. Heading to Kansas City, he lived with a former fellow inmate for a short time. But law enforcement officials kept a close eye on the ex-convict, much to Charley's chagrin. During 1929 local police arrested him six times, "pending investigation," and usually released him after one night in jail. As Charley later explained to a newspaper reporter, "I'm not as bad as they say I am. They just wouldn't let me alone after I got out."

By the end of 1929, Charley had relocated to Akron, Ohio, working with a gang of ex-cons that he had met in prison. The bandits robbed several places near Toledo during the first few months of 1930, but their biggest robbery took place at the Farmers & Merchants Bank of Sylvania, Ohio, on February 5. Though they escaped with two thousand dollars, three members of the group—including Charley—were subsequently arrested for the murder of an Akron police officer during a robbery on March 8.

During the murder investigation, Akron police discovered that Charley had not been a participant in the policeman's murder. But before he could be released from the Akron jail, police officers arrived from Toledo to arrest him for the Sylvania, Ohio, bank robbery. After Charley's transfer to Toledo, two bank employees and two customers positively identified him as one of the Sylvania bank robbers.

On November 24, 1930, Charley and another gang member were sentenced to serve twelve to fifteen years at the Ohio State Penitentiary in Columbus for the Sylvania bank job. Handcuffed and escorted by two deputies on the evening of December 10, Charley and two other prisoners boarded a train in Toledo for transfer to the Columbus prison.

During the train ride to Toledo, Charley persistently requested to go to the lavatory. Afraid he would try to get away, deputies denied his request. After the train made a routine stop at Kenton to pick up passengers, however, deputies agreed he could go to the lavatory once the train pulled out of the Kenton station. Charley, who was handcuffed to Nathan King, another prisoner, led the way into the lavatory.

"They hadn't been inside more than ten seconds before we heard a window crash," Deputy Joe Packo later explained. "I . . .

rushed in and found King standing alone with the handcuffs dangling at his side. The window was smashed. Floyd was gone."

Charley had jumped from the train only ten miles before reaching the state prison. Though the deputies notified the Kenton police about their prisoner's sensational escape, Charley's freedom was already well underway.

Throughout 1931 and 1932 Charley supposedly committed at last half of all the bank robberies in Oklahoma, often working in tandem with other well-known criminals. In 1931 alone, fifty-one Oklahoma banks were robbed, and the name of Pretty Boy Floyd graced the front pages of Oklahoma newspapers almost daily. As one headline screamed, "Pretty Boy Pretty Bad, Says Banker."

Bankers demanded that the Oklahoma governor call out the National Guard to hunt down Pretty Boy. Though acting governor Robert Burns declined to employ the National Guard for the hunt, he issued a statement on January 15, 1932, revealing that the state and the Oklahoma Bankers' Association were offering a combined reward totaling six thousand dollars for the capture of Charles Arthur "Pretty Boy" Floyd.

Within a week Burns received a letter from Charley that stated, "Robert Burns, Acting Governor—you will either withdraw that one thousand dollar reward at once or suffer the consequences—no kidding. I have robbed no one but the monied men."

Charley's statement about robbing only "monied men" helped cement his reputation as a modern-day Robin Hood among many Oklahoma residents. Some of the state's citizens loved telling stories of Charley ripping up mortgage papers during bank robberies to prevent unscrupulous bankers from stealing land from poor farmers. By some accounts he was feeding at least a dozen families with stolen cash, and he became widely known throughout Oklahoma as "The Phantom of the Ozarks" and "The King of the Bank Robbers."

As his crime spree continued, national interest in Charley reached a peak on June 17, 1933, in Kansas City, Missouri. Now known as the "Kansas City Massacre," the event was an attempt by Pretty Boy Floyd, Vernon Miller, and Adam Richetti to free their friend, Frank Nash, from law enforcement officials. At the time, Frank Nash was at the Union Railway Station, returning to the US penitentiary at Leavenworth, Kansas, under heavily armed escorts. Charley and his friends blasted machine gun fire as soon as four police officers appeared with their prisoner outside the station. All five men were killed.

Unscathed, Charley and Adam Richetti escaped from the massacre. In early September 1933, they met two women in Toledo, Ohio, and asked the pair to accompany them to Buffalo, New York. While the couples kept a low profile in their New York hideaway, they learned that the notorious criminal John Dillinger was gunned down on July 23, 1934, in Chicago—and that FBI director J. Edgar Hoover had named Pretty Boy Floyd as "Public Enemy Number One" following John Dillinger's death.

By October 1934 the couples agreed to return to Oklahoma. The four set out early on Saturday morning, October 20. A few hours into their journey, Charley encountered heavy fog and skidded their automobile into a telephone pole near Wellsville, Ohio. Removing their firearms from the vehicle, the two men remained on the side of the road while the women took the damaged car into a Wellsville garage for repairs.

Wellsville police chief J. H. Fultz soon received a phone call from a local farmer who had seen two strange men on a hillside on the outskirts of town. The police chief and two other officers immediately went to the scene and found the men resting in a wooded area. As Chief Fultz approached the strangers, one of the men pulled out a gun and shot at the officer. The shooter's companion took off, running up the hill and firing at the law enforcement officials.

The local police took the remaining man into custody. Although the prisoner initially gave a false name, he was eventually identified as Adam Richetti. He maintained that the escaped bandit was a Toledo man named James Warren, but Chief Fultz was convinced that the man on the loose was none other than Pretty Boy Floyd.

Meanwhile, Charley had flagged down a motorist from East Liverpool in an attempt to get as far away as possible from the shooting scene. When the car ran out of gas, he grabbed another ride with a Wellsville florist. Different stories have emerged about the events that followed, but Charley's unwilling chauffeur apparently slowed the car to a crawl as they approached a roadblock that had been set up by local authorities. Charley ordered the driver to turn around and head back down the road. A Lisbon police officer and a sheriff's deputy quickly set out after the car. Some accounts contend that Charley broke out the rear window of the automobile and opened fire on the pursuing vehicle before fleeing into the woods. Other versions of the story claim that no bullets were fired before Charley leaped out of the car and disappeared.

By the end of the day, police, deputies, and armed citizens were combing every inch of Columbiana County for Public Enemy Number One. Moreover, federal agents had been notified and were headed to Ohio to join the pursuit.

The search continued on Sunday, October 21, but Charley eluded searchers for nearly forty-eight hours. The beginning of the end for Pretty Boy Floyd arrived when a farmer noticed him walking through the area near Ellen Conkle's farmhouse in Sprucevale. Acting on the tip, four local police officers and five federal agents set out for the Conkle farm. By Monday afternoon, October 22, 1934, Charles Arthur Floyd had been apprehended and killed. He was thirty years old.

In the end, Charley had murdered ten people and robbed dozens of banks. His final partner, Adam Richetti, was eventually returned to Kansas City. Convicted of murder, he became the first man to die in Missouri's gas chamber.

Five years after Floyd's death, musician Woody Guthrie, an Oklahoma native, romanticized Floyd's life by writing the song, "The Ballad of Pretty Boy Floyd." Since that time the song has been recorded by many musicians, including Guthrie's son, Arlo. Moreover, numerous books and films have been issued about the outlaw's life over the years, continuing the public's fascination with Pretty Boy Floyd.

Anna Marie Hahn

Arsenic Anna
1906–1938

Cincinnati police first heard of Anna Marie Hahn in early August 1937. A telegram arrived at police headquarters, sent by detectives in Colorado Springs, Colorado, with a request to bring in the Cincinnati woman for questioning.

As the message explained, the co-owner of the Park Hotel in Colorado Springs had discovered one of the hotel's guests, Anna Marie Hahn, in her private quarters at the hotel. She immediately chased the guest out of the room. It wasn't until Hahn had checked out of the hotel that the proprietor noticed that two diamond rings were missing from her dresser. Upon the realization that Hahn, a Cincinnati resident, may have stolen the rings, the hotel operator reported the theft to the police.

Moreover, Colorado detectives discovered the same woman had apparently dropped off a sick man at a local hospital and then mysteriously disappeared. The gentleman, a resident of Cincinnati by the name of George Obendorfer, had died alone at the Colorado Springs hospital on August 1, 1937.

At the time, Cincinnati police must have thought they would be dealing solely with a case of grand larceny. Little did anyone realize that the robbery report would lead police to a string of mysterious deaths in Cincinnati, all involving elderly men who had been associated with Anna Marie Hahn. And no one could have predicted that Hahn would be convicted of murdering numerous Ohio men— and become the first woman in Ohio to die in the electric chair.

Hahn was the youngest of twelve children, born on July 7, 1906, in Fuessen, Germany, as Anna Marie Filser. Her parents were

Anna Marie Hahn
OHIO HISTORY CONNECTION

respected, devout Catholics who gave their guidance and support to all their children. At age seventeen Hahn fell in love with a married man who was reportedly a Viennese physician. When Hahn informed her lover that she was pregnant, he revealed to her that he was already married. The man suggested she have an abortion—which promptly ended the relationship. Hahn later claimed that she did not know about his wife in the beginning of their relationship.

When Hahn's family learned she was going to have a child out of wedlock, they sent her to Holland to live with one of her sisters until she gave birth. After the baby, Oscar, was born in 1925, Hahn returned to Germany. Back at home she soon discovered she could not tolerate the gossip about her status as an unwed mother. In 1928 she wrote to her step-uncle, Max Doeschel, a retired carpenter residing in Cincinnati, told him that she wanted to come to the United States, and asked him for a loan to finance her travels.

At age twenty-two Hahn immigrated to the United States, arriving in New York on February 12, 1929. Living with her step-uncle in Cincinnati, she had little trouble finding work as a housekeeper at a local hotel. She also maintained an active social life, attending German dances in the community. At one dance she met a Western Union telegrapher by the name of Philip Hahn. He soon proposed, and she agreed to marry him on the condition that she could bring her son from Germany to live with them.

About three months after Anna Marie Filser met Philip Hahn, the couple married on May 5, 1930, in Buffalo, New York. In July of that year, Hahn went to Germany and brought Oscar, who was approximately six years old, to the United States. Though the couple started their own businesses in Cincinnati, a restaurant and a bakery, both failed due to the poor economic environment following the stock market crash in 1929.

Life looked brighter for the family when Hahn inherited a house in Cincinnati from an elderly German man, Ernest Kohler, after his death in 1933. Kohler was reportedly a childhood friend of Hahn's father and chose to name Hahn as his benefactor. The house was valued at approximately twelve thousand dollars.

In spite of inheriting Kohler's house, the Hahns' financial situation looked grim as Philip remained unemployed. Worried about finances, Anna started gambling in hopes of improving her finances. She tried her hand at the gaming tables across the river in Newport, and she loved to gamble on horse races, frequenting the track three or four times a week.

An attractive blonde with a thick German accent, Hahn also realized that she could easily find men who would be flattered by the attentions of a kind, attractive young woman—especially men with financial means. In 1936 she met George Heis, a coal dealer, and borrowed money from him to make good on her losses on racehorse bets. When Heis's coal supplier pressed him to pay his bill, he demanded Hahn repay the money he had loaned to her.

Without the funds to pay off the loan, Hahn used her feminine wiles to stall the repayment by cooking for him. After eating one of the meals that Hahn had prepared, however, Heis became violently ill. Though he recovered, the mysterious illness left him partially paralyzed.

With Heis unable to work, the coal supplier turned to Hahn directly for repayment of the money that she owed Heis. Still lacking the means to repay the loan, Hahn turned to another elderly gentleman for help. Soon after meeting Albert Palmer, a seventy-two-year-old retired railroad watchman with a small pension, Hahn prepared several meals for him at his home. She also convinced him to loan thirteen hundred dollars to her and used part of the funds to pay the coal company. Within days of lending the money to Hahn, however, Palmer became seriously ill. He died on March 27, 1937, of unknown causes.

Heis's devastating illness and Palmer's death apparently emboldened Hahn to seek out more victims for her deadly schemes. A few months after Palmer died, Hahn met Jacob Wagner, a seventy-eight-year-old retired gardener. Hahn later claimed she met Wagner when he came to her house and told her he believed they were related. Wagner's neighbors, however, insisted Hahn had gone to Wagner's apartment building and asked if "any old German men" resided in the complex.

Hahn visited Wagner in his one-room quarters on June 2, 1937. He died the following day. The next morning Hahn arrived at Wagner's bank with a check that had been signed by Wagner, payable to her. Hahn explained to the bank that he had written the check so she would have some money to pay his bills. Several days later she went to the probate court to gain access to Wagner's residence. Accompanied by a court deputy, Hahn entered Wagner's home and retrieved a will. The terms of the document left all of Wagner's property to Hahn.

Not long after Wagner's death, Hahn met another German man, George Gsellman. On July 6, 1937, only one day after Hahn cooked a meal for the man in his attic room, he died. Authorities would later reveal that food left in Gsellman's room contained enough poison to kill three or four people.

Less than a month after Gsellman's death, Hahn met George Obendorfer, sixty-seven, a German cobbler who was described as "well-to-do." Not many days after meeting, Hahn and Obendorfer left Cincinnati, headed for Colorado with Hahn's young son, Oscar. Before leaving, Hahn signed Wagner's name to a check for one thousand dollars. She later insisted she needed the money and knew Wagner would want her to have it.

The trio got off the train in Colorado Springs and checked into a local hotel. After eating a meal that Hahn had prepared for him, Obendorfer abruptly became ill. Hahn took him to a local hospital, telling registration officials that the man was a stranger she had met on the train, and quickly returned to the hotel. Obendorfer died at the hospital on August 1, 1937.

The reported theft of jewels at the Colorado Springs hotel was the beginning of the end for Hahn, and all her actions over the previous few months began to unravel. When Cincinnati detectives took Anna Marie Hahn into custody at the request of Colorado Springs detectives, she readily admitted that she had visited Colorado with her son. But she denied traveling with Obendorfer until she suddenly "remembered" she had run into him in Chicago and sat with him on the train during the next leg of the journey. She also admitted that he had become very sick after she fed him at the hotel.

While Hahn was being questioned, another detective noticed the attractive woman and recognized her name. A local restaurant owner had notified police earlier about the sudden death of a regular patron, Jacob Wagner, and had reported that one of Wagner's friends had been Anna Marie Hahn.

After three hours of interrogation, Hahn was locked up in the county jail. Cincinnati police launched their official investigation by questioning Hahn's husband, Philip, at the Hahns' home. He claimed he had known nothing about his wife's trip to Colorado Springs until he found a note that she had left for him on the kitchen table.

But Philip admitted he and his wife had argued over a bottle of poison that her son, Oscar, had found in the basement, which he turned over to police. Moreover, Philip revealed that Hahn had stolen blank prescription forms from a physician's office, forged the doctor's signature, and ordered poisons from a local drugstore. She even sent her son to the store to pick up the prescriptions, but the druggist refused to turn over the drugs to the young boy due to his age.

During a search of the Hahns' residence, investigators found a small bottle hidden between the rafters between the first floor and the cellar. Hahn repeatedly demanded that detectives return the bottle to her, claiming it must belong to her son's chemistry set, but the investigators refused to relinquish the item. Testing later confirmed that the white, powdery substance in the bottle contained more than seventy grams of arsenic trioxide.

As the investigation continued, police discovered that two more elderly gentleman in Cincinnati—Palmer and Gsellman—had died of sudden, mysterious ailments in recent months, and both men had connections to Hahn.

The state elected to prosecute Hahn only for the alleged murder of Wagner by proving that "Wagner's death was only one of a series of planned poison murders through which . . . [Hahn] sought to enrich herself . . . for profit." In spite of strenuous objections from the defense, the judge ruled the prosecution could refer to Hahn's association "with a number of older men."

In screening potential jurors, the prosecution clearly established that the jury would be asked to send Hahn to the electric chair. At age thirty-one Hahn went on trial for her life on October 11, 1937, only two months and one day after her arrest. She proclaimed her innocence to the court, pleading not guilty to the charges.

The prosecution presented multiple experts to establish the cause of Wagner's death. Medical experts testified that Wagner had died from a "tremendous dose of arsenic." Moreover, a toxicologist said arsenic probably was the primary factor contributing to the death of Albert Palmer. In a graphic display of evidence, medical experts exhibited the two men's poisoned vital organs in large fiber boxes in the courtroom.

The prosecution also submitted Hahn's white knitted purse as evidence, which yielded particles containing 35 percent arsenic. Hahn had brought the purse with her to the police station at the time of her arrest. Though the prosecution also insisted Obendorfer had died in Colorado from food that had been salted with shakers that contained 8 percent arsenic trioxide, the judge would not allow the shakers to be submitted as evidence.

A handwriting expert claimed Hahn had forged Wagner's will, supplying a monetary motive linking Hahn with the murder of Wagner. But the most dramatic moment occurred during the second week of the trial when George Heis arrived in the courthouse to testify for the prosecution. Testifying from his wheelchair, Heis claimed Hahn had bilked him out of more than two thousand dollars. According to his testimony, Hahn had told him she would place an inheritance from her uncle in Heis's name if he would pay the taxes on the funds. Hahn often prepared meals for him, Heis explained. But after eating a feast of chicken and spinach that she had cooked, Heis became violently ill and eventually was paralyzed. He also noted that the spinach had tasted sweet, a characteristic of food flavored with arsenic.

Heis ended his testimony by looking directly at Hahn and pointing a gnarled finger at her. "She did this to me," he claimed.

During the trial the *Cincinnati Enquirer* used vivid details to describe Hahn's role in killing four men and paralyzing another gentleman, as well as her testimony on the witness stand. In describing Albert Palmer, Hahn claimed he was like a father to her and her son, the newspaper reported. She even used the term, "My Dear Sweet Daddy," as a salutation on a letter to him.

Along with the *Cincinnati Enquirer*, the courtroom was packed with other news outlets that provided coverage of the trial across the nation. Headlines in the *Chicago Tribune* dubbed Hahn as "Arsenic Anna." One newspaper described Hahn as a "poker-faced, blonde German woman who at no time displayed any appearance of resentment or shock at anything that has been said."

Reporter Virginia Gardner of the *Chicago Tribune* focused many of her articles on the dress and appearance of Hahn, the eleven women of the jury, and the sole male juror, who was named foreman of the group. In fact, Gardner's coverage often resembled a story about a fashion show. She described one juror as wearing "a tightly fitting burnt orange suit with a round collar," and another wearing "a colorful blouse."

In one lengthy description about Hahn, she wrote, "Her bright hair, brighter on top than the strands showing through, was elaborately and freshly curled. . . . Her cold pale blue eyes were arched over brows scarcely darkened by an eyebrow pencil. She wore a conservative tailored suit of navy blue, a high-necked demure white blouse, sheer stockings, and high heeled pumps." On several occasions she wrote that Hahn wore "a brown crepe dress with tiny birds of gold poised in flight." In another article Gardner called Hahn the "blonde defendant, whose ankles are slender and shapely, but whose skirts are long."

The press also uncovered other possible poison victims. While caring for Julia Kresckay, forty-eight, of Cincinnati, during a brief illness, Hahn borrowed eight hundred dollars from the woman. When Hahn did not repay the loan, Kresckay threatened to prosecute her. Within a short time Kresckay became severely ill and was paralyzed as a result of the illness.

Another Cincinnati woman, Ollie Luella Koehler, seventy-nine, died on August 19, 1937, at Longview State Hospital, after eating ice cream that Hahn had given her on July 10. Police later found a bag in Hahn's home that contained Koehler's valuables and a signed document that named "Mrs. A. Filser"—Hahn's maiden name—as the power of attorney for Koehler.

In all, ninety-six witnesses testified for the prosecution at the trial. In contrast, only three witnesses—Hahn, Oscar, and a Chicago toxicologist—appeared for the defense. The toxicologist claimed that the symptoms of all the victims could be attributed to many other reasons besides arsenic. Little Oscar testified that he never saw his mother put anything in Obendorfer's food. He also claimed that many of the little bottles in the basement of his home belonged to his chemistry set. At the same time he admitted that he and his father had found a bottle of poison in the basement that did not belong to him.

After her son's testimony Hahn took the stand in her own defense. She continued to proclaim her innocence during two days of testimony, flatly denying any guilt and claiming that the string of witnesses had not told the truth.

The jury received the case shortly after nine o'clock on Friday evening, November 5. They deliberated for nearly an hour before retiring for the night. After a little more than two hours of deliberation the next morning, the jury reached a verdict.

Back in the courtroom the jury foreman announced a guilty verdict with no recommendation for mercy. Hahn stood passively before the judge as he sentenced her to death. Though she walked out of the courtroom with a steady gait, she crumbled as she waited on the elevator. When Hahn reached the women's quarters, she collapsed and fainted.

The defense immediately filed a motion for a new trial, citing multiple errors. The judge denied the motion, stating "the evidence was so overwhelming that no verdict other than guilty could have been reached by the jury."

Her counsel appealed to the Ohio Court of Appeals for Hamilton County, which ruled that Hahn had a fair trial and no error intervened with prejudice. The Ohio Supreme Court and the US Supreme Court also refused to consider her case.

Since clemency from Governor Martin Davey was Hahn's last hope of escaping the electric chair, her defense counsel requested and received a clemency hearing. At the hearing Hahn's attorney pleaded for her life to be spared. Even Oscar appealed to the governor, saying Hahn had been "as good a mother as there is."

But Governor Davey refused to intervene. Although he admitted he detested the thought of allowing a woman to go to the chair, he had no choice but to permit the decision of the courts to stand because Hahn's crimes were "so cold-blooded, so deliberately planned and executed."

Until the hour before her death, Hahn maintained her innocence. Shortly before her execution, however, Hahn presented several letters to her attorneys. In the letters she confessed to the crimes, detailing her actions and motives in much the same way that the prosecution had claimed.

Hahn, described by the press as "a pitiful, whimpering creature," went to the electric chair shortly after 8:00 p.m. on December 7, 1938. As she entered the death chamber, she took only a few steps before collapsing to the floor and begging the warden, "Please don't let them do this to me."

But her pleas were too late. In the middle of repeating the Lord's Prayer, Anna Maria Hahn was electrocuted for her crimes, becoming the first woman in Ohio to die in the electric chair.

Edythe Klumpp

Murderous Seamstress
1918–1999

The reporter leaned forward and shoved a microphone into the face of a neatly dressed woman with short, curly blonde hair. "What would you like to see as far as a verdict from the jury in this case?" the reporter asked.

After testifying on the witness stand for more than three and a half hours, the woman appeared drained and forlorn. "Naturally, I would like to see not guilty," she responded in a soft tone.

"Not guilty?" the reporter repeated. "Would you feel it would be a fair verdict if they returned, say, a manslaughter verdict in this case?"

"I feel like I'm not guilty," she managed to say.

Across the nation, viewers were transfixed by the black-and-white images flickering across their television screens in the summer of 1959. A former Sunday school teacher and the mother of four, Edythe Klumpp hardly seemed to fit the profile of a cold-blooded murderer. But the Cincinnati native had been charged with the brutal murder of her boyfriend's wife and was now fighting for her own life.

Days after the television interview, the jury reached a verdict: guilty. As Edythe awaited sentencing, the television reporter interviewed her again from the Ohio Reformatory for Women in Marysville. Her fingers constantly fidgeted with a handkerchief, and she admitted she was extremely nervous as she waited for the judge's decision. After a few moments of discussion about her general health and her children attending summer camp, the reporter

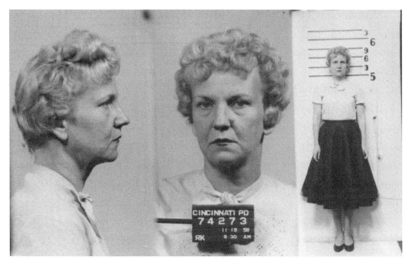

Edythe Klumpp

asked, "Have your opinions changed at all about the verdict since the trial's been over?"

"No," she replied softly, but firmly. "I'm innocent of it."

Edythe's insistence of her innocence, however, did not dissuade Judge Frank M. Gusweiler of Hamilton County Pleas Court. The judge issued the harshest penalty allowed and sentenced her to die on December 15, 1959. But who was this killer who maintained she was not guilty of murder? And what dire circumstances had led to her trial and conviction?

By all indications Edythe's early life held no hints of the murderous act in her future. Born on January 15, 1918, Edith Margaret Reis was the daughter of Harry "Jack" Reis, a steamfitter who once played professional baseball for the St. Louis Cardinals. Little is known about her mother other than that her maiden name was Fann. Edith, as her name was spelled at birth, grew up in Cincinnati and actively participated in sports as a student at Hartwell High School. After high school graduation she took a job as a playground supervisor and assistant gym teacher for the National Youth Association.

Edith continued working after she married George Montgomery in 1936, but resigned from her job when she became pregnant a short time later. The couple's only son, Jack, was born in 1938. Two years later the Montgomerys divorced, and Edith was awarded custody of her son.

But Edith would not remain a single mother for long. A few months after her divorce was finalized, Edith met a gentleman by the name of Robert "Bob" Klumpp, who worked as a printer. The couple soon married and started their family. They eventually had two boys and two girls. Their second child, a son, died at the tender age of six months.

The Klumpps had been married only a few years when they opened their home to foster children. During World War II they provided foster care for as many as fifteen children in their Cincinnati home. Licensed by both the state and county to serve as foster parents, the couple was recognized as one of the outstanding foster families in Hamilton County.

In 1952 the Klumpps built a home together in Mount Washington, located in the Cincinnati suburbs. Even though money was tight, they obtained loans from at least two banks and borrowed funds from Edith's mother to finance their primary residence. The Klumpps were active and regular members of the Norwood English Lutheran Church, where Edith taught Sunday school, was a co-advisor to the Lutheran League, and sang in the choir.

With mounting debts from the move, Edith returned to work outside the home. She was dismissed from several jobs—including one as a clerk at a clothing store and another position at the state highway patrol—for bad work habits. She did find success as a sewing instructor, holding classes during weeknights at several schools. In September 1954 she took a job as a waitress at the Sky Galley restaurant at Lunken Airport. During this period she also started using the Old English spelling of "Edythe" for her first name.

To the outside world the churchgoing Klumpps, who had been honored by the community for their role as foster parents, were leading exemplary lives. But the private world of Bob and Edythe Klumpp apparently was much different behind closed doors. In 1956 Edythe brought assault and battery charges against her husband and headed to a local law firm to begin divorce proceedings.

During an interview with Cincinnati detectives, Bob later claimed troubles erupted in the marriage soon after Edythe started work at Sky Galley. He blamed one of her coworkers for encouraging Edythe to dye her hair blonde and accompany her to dances, where they would meet up with men. Bob also revealed he had proof that Edythe had several boyfriends, and he had communicated with the wife of one of the men on numerous occasions.

Edythe's sister-in-law, Mrs. John Rogers, also revealed to the *Cincinnati Enquirer* that Edythe's appearance changed drastically after the family moved to Mount Washington. "She never used to spend money [to buy clothes], but shortly before she and Bob were divorced, she had her hair blonded [and] bought up a lot of clothes," she explained, adding that her sister-in-law had changed from a "dumpy woman to a good-looking one."

After seventeen years of marriage, the Klumpps finalized their divorce in August 1957. As part of the divorce settlement, they agreed to sell the house, and Bob would receive six thousand dollars of the proceeds. Although Edythe listed the house with a real estate agent on the condition that she would make necessary improvements and repairs, she failed to live up to her end of the bargain. As a result the house was never shown to prospective buyers.

Apparently Edythe was much too busy working—and seeing various men—to devote any time to sprucing up the house. In March 1958 she met a young gentleman at Sky Galley who was dining at the restaurant after a flying lesson. Ten years her junior, William "Bill" Bergen pursued the blonde, twice-divorced waitress, and Edythe and Bill were soon involved in an intimate relationship.

Edythe would later admit that she knew, from the start of the relationship, that Bill was married with a young daughter. But he had insisted, she claimed, that he was getting a divorce from Louise Bergen, who was living in a nearby apartment with their daughter, Linda.

Louise Bergen and Edythe Klumpp met each other for the first time when Louise borrowed Bill's car to go to a funeral. Edythe drove Bill to the apartment parking lot to wait for Louise to return home. When Bill introduced the two women, Edythe was surprised by Louise's friendliness. Louise insisted that she had been anxious to meet Edythe and was happy to finally meet her.

Bill soon moved into Edythe's home, even giving her an eight-dollar ring and a promise to eventually marry her. The couple exchanged private—although not legal—vows, and Edythe started telling everyone that they were husband and wife.

As Bill and Edythe made plans for a future together, Edythe decided that it would be better to keep her home in Mount Washington and borrow money to pay off her ex-husband for his share of the proceeds from the sale. Bob Klumpp agreed to the proposal, even conceding to take four thousand dollars in cash instead of the original six thousand dollars. According to Edythe her boyfriend was more than willing to cosign a loan on the house instead of selling it. When they signed the loan papers to borrow a total of nine thousand dollars, however, Edythe's signature—"Mrs. Bergen"—bore no resemblance to her legal name.

Throughout the summer of 1958, Bill and Edythe lived in Mount Washington with her children as a family, often taking the youngsters on outings and to sporting activities. The couple even slipped off by themselves for a few days in August to take a "honeymoon" at a state park in Indiana. On several occasions throughout the summer and early fall, Edythe also crossed paths with Louise Bergen. By Edythe's account Louise remained friendly and polite and did not seem surprised that she and Bill were planning to get legally married within the next year or two.

But everything changed for Edythe Klumpp and Bill and Louise Bergen on November 1, 1958. Duck hunters on the shores of Cowan Lake in Clinton County were packing up for the day, ready to head home, when they stumbled across a woman's charred body in the cattails surrounding the lake. The men could see a pair of blistered legs with the remains of some nylon stockings and a piece of red cloth over the head. They also saw a broken gold necklace around the throat, but the rest of the remains were charred and wet from the drizzly weather. Once the sheriff arrived on the scene and the body was taken to the morgue, they discovered several keys and a small penknife attached to a key ring under the body. The next day another inspection turned up two rings: a plain band and a ring with some diamonds.

On the same day the body was discovered, William Bergen reported that his wife, Louise, was missing. Louise, age thirty-two, had short, brown hair, stood about five feet, nine inches tall, and weighed about 140 pounds. She was last seen wearing a red coat as she left work at 5:00 p.m. on Thursday, October 30.

By Tuesday, November 4, Cincinnati detectives had confirmed that the charred remains belonged to Louise Bergen. Her death was ruled a homicide. Following his wife's murder, William was brought in for questioning. An initial lie detector test was inconclusive, with Bill claiming he was nervous. A few days later he repeated the test and passed the exam.

After police interviewed Edythe several times at her home, she was asked to come to the police station for more questions. Edythe drove herself to police headquarters in her own car. Investigators immediately searched the automobile and found traces of blood on the front seat. When a lie detector test indicated Edythe was exhibiting deception, she became the prime suspect in the case. Told about the test and the bloodstains, Edythe began to talk.

Edythe admitted that she agreed to meet Bill's estranged wife at Swifton Village Shopping Center on October 30 to discuss whether Louise was planning to divorce William. Louise got into Edythe's car around 5:30 p.m. Wanting a quiet place to talk, they drove to Caldwell Park in Hartwell.

After parking the car, Edythe tried to push back the seat to be more comfortable for their conversation. When the seat wouldn't budge, she got out of the car, looked in the back seat, and found a bottle wedged into the cushion. When she stood upright, Louise was pointing a gun at her. Edythe told police the weapon was Bill's pistol, which she had left in the front seat because she had been taking target practice.

Edythe grabbed for the gun. The two women struggled. The gun accidentally went off, firing into Louise's throat. Louise collapsed, lifelessly, onto the front seat. Panicking, Edythe claimed she dragged the body to the back of the car and placed it into the trunk. Then she drove away, throwing Louise's purse and the gun out the window.

With Louise still in the trunk, Edythe returned home for a brief time to change out of her bloody clothes before setting off for Woodward High School to teach a sewing class. The next day she cleaned the car, filled a can of gas at the Mt. Washington Service Station, drove to Cowan Lake, and burned the body.

Edythe's signed confession, along with the physical evidence, was enough for police to arrest her for first-degree murder.

Hamilton County prosecutor C. Watson Hover soon discovered that Edythe had cosigned a loan application with Bill Bergen under the name of "Mrs. Bergen." According to his reasoning Edythe's fraudulent loan application was a motiving factor in her decision to eliminate the real Mrs. Bergen. The prosecutor believed he had everything he needed to obtain a conviction for premeditated murder: a confession, blood evidence, and a motive.

In the months leading up to the trial, William visited Edythe in jail, often staying for hours at a time. But by late February the visits stopped. Bergen quit his job and moved to Washington, DC, with a new, nineteen-year-old girlfriend.

William "Foss" Hopkins, Edythe's attorney, urged her to change her statement. Edythe refused, continuing to claim she was not guilty of first-degree murder. Louise's death, she insisted, was the result of an accidental shooting.

The murder trial began in June 1959 in the courtroom of Judge Frank M. Gusweiler of Hamilton County Pleas Court. Foss

Hopkins tried to get Edythe's confession thrown out of court, arguing that police failed to comply with her request for a lawyer and coerced a confession with promises of leniency. Even though Edythe took the stand in her defense and stated that investigators had promised she would be charged with manslaughter, the judge ruled that her confession would stand.

During the trial Edythe was on the witness stand for two days. Hopkins attempted to deflect guilt on Bill Bergen, who testified he gave Edythe an informal engagement ring but always intended to return to his wife. In Hopkins's closing statement, he said, "I have come to the conclusion that we are trying the wrong party. The man . . . who caused this tragedy has been permitted to go scot-free . . . by his deceit, subterfuge and honey-dripping promises and vows."

His argument, however, failed to convince the jury of Edythe's innocence. After nineteen days of testimony, the jury found Edythe guilty of first-degree murder without recommendation for mercy. "Without mercy" meant no leniency for sentencing.

While awaiting formal sentencing in the Hamilton County jail, and knowing she could face execution, Edythe changed her story about the murder. Speaking to a clergyman, she told a much different story from the events in her confession and put the blame squarely on Bill Bergen. Bill contrived the original story, she claimed, and threatened to harm her children if she connected him with Louise's death.

In this new version of the story, Edythe said Bill was also present in the car on the evening of the murder. Although they had picked up Louise at the shopping center, they did not go to Caldwell Park. Instead they drove to a secluded, wooded area on Stratton Drive in Anderson Township, located in Clinton County. As Bill and Louise argued, Edythe went into the woods to relieve herself. By the time she returned to the car, Louise had been shot. Bill claimed the shooting was accidental. Together, she and Bill put the body in the trunk and went directly to Cowan Lake that evening to burn the body.

Although Hopkins presented Edythe's revised statement to the court, hoping for a new trial, the judge was not swayed and sentenced Edythe to die on December 15, 1959. While Edythe awaited execution in the Ohio Reformatory for Women in Marysville, Hopkins unsuccessfully appealed the verdict all the way to the US Supreme Court. In one last effort Hopkins made a direct appeal to Ohio governor Michael V. DiSalle.

DiSalle, who had just been elected to office, did not hide the fact that he opposed capital punishment. He decided to grant Edythe a thirty-day stay of execution until he and the parole board could review the case. In a presentation to the board, Hopkins even offered to administer a truth serum to Edythe. Still, the board denied the appeal.

Hopkins's arguments, however, must have had a profound impact on the Ohio governor. Unbeknownst to anyone, DiSalle traveled to the Marysville prison two days before the rescheduled execution. Accompanying him was a psychiatry professor from Ohio State University. At the prison Edythe was given sodium amytal. During a two-hour interview with DiSalle, she retold her revised story, saying it was Bergen who accidentally killed his wife and came up with the plan to burn the body.

Convinced Edythe was telling the truth, DiSalle commuted Klumpp's sentence to life in prison. By ignoring the jury's verdict, the governor's decision caused an uproar with the public and the press. In his own defense he penned a letter to the editor of the *Cincinnati Enquirer*. At the same time, several newspapers printed the transcript of Edythe's truth serum interview for the public to read.

After reading the newspaper transcripts, Irwin Schulte, a deputy sheriff who helped investigate the case, stepped forward with some new information. On the night of Louise's death, Schulte recalled that Anderson Township rangers found some eyeglasses, bloodstained shorts, and a piece of a broken necklace on Stratton Drive. Since no one connected the items to the Bergen case, which everyone believed had taken place miles away in

Hamilton County, the rangers turned over the items to Clinton County officials.

Investigators rechecked the evidence and discovered that the pieces of necklace found on Stratton Drive matched the broken necklace found on Louise's body. They also determined that the glasses were the same type of eyeglasses worn by Louise.

Although Governor DiSalle requested that the prosecutor reopen the investigation and question Bill Bergan again, Hover refused. Determined to find a way around the prosecution's lack of cooperation, the governor ordered an investigation by the Ohio State Patrol. The patrol's investigation determined that Louise was killed on Stratton Drive, and her body was burned on the night of her death. Though Bill had initially claimed he was at a friend's home on the evening of Louise's death, he suddenly changed his alibi by telling the patrol he had really been with a prostitute. Upon further investigation the woman admitted Bill had visited her—but not on the evening of Louise's murder. Despite the new report, however, the prosecutor would not consider reopening the case.

In 1962 Governor DiSalle was defeated in his reelection bid by James A. Rhodes. Voters claimed that DiSalle's personal involvement in the Klumpp case and his defiance in ignoring the jury's recommendations convinced them not to reelect the governor for a second term.

But DiSalle had the final word on the Klumpp case. On his last day in the governor's office, the governor commuted Edythe's sentence to second-degree murder, making her eligible for parole. As he explained to the *Cincinnati Enquirer*, "All I think she was guilty of was perjury rather than murder." Though he rebuked Edythe for her actions and lies, he placed the blame for the murder solely on William Bergen.

Edythe served eleven years of her sentence in the Ohio Reformatory for Women in Marysville. During her incarceration she gave sewing lessons to other prisoners, participated in a singing group, and worked with medical records in the prison hospital.

Edythe Klumpp was released from prison on May 12, 1971. She refused to make any statement to the press upon her release. Even after moving into the Batavia home of one of her daughters, she never publicly commented on her case. As her daughter told the press, "There is no chance of talking to my mother. She wants to remain private."

By 1975 Edythe was living in an Anderson Township apartment building, and her name was no longer being mentioned in the press. She remarried in 1976 and moved to southern Kentucky with her new husband. She died of natural causes on December 24, 1999, at the age of eighty-one.

Jean Struven Harris

The Scorned Headmistress
1923-2012

In New York's Westchester County Courthouse, the judge looked down from his bench and asked a woman with pale blonde hair if she had anything to say before he passed sentence on her.

Jean Struven Harris met the judge's gaze with defiance blazing from her blue eyes. "I want to say that I did not murder Herman Tarnower; that I loved him very much, and I never wished him ill, and I am innocent as I stand here. For you or for Mr. Bolen [the prosecutor] to arrange my life so that I will be in a cage for the rest of it, and that every time I walk outside, I will have iron around my wrists, is not justice. It is a travesty of justice."

Her passionate plea failed to sway the judge into giving her a lighter sentence than normal. On March 20, 1981, Jean Struven Harris, a highly respected educator and former lover of Dr. Herman Tarnower, received the maximum sentence of fifteen years to life for the second-degree murder of the esteemed cardiologist.

Jean testified in court that she had intended to end her life on March 10, 1980, after bidding goodbye to her lover of fourteen years. But it was Dr. Tarnower—not Jean Harris—who died of gunshot wounds that evening. She claimed it was an accident, stemming from a struggle as the doctor tried to remove the gun from her hands.

The jury of eight women and four men did not believe her story. On February 28, 1981, the jury foreman announced that the Smith College graduate was guilty of second-degree murder. After sentencing she headed to New York's Bedford Hills Correctional

Jean Harris
THE MADEIRA SCHOOL

Facility for Women, and the upper-middle-class life of Jean Harris came to a screeching halt.

Fifteen years in prison was not the life that young Jean had envisioned for herself. Born on April 27, 1923, Jean Witte Struven grew up in the fashionable suburbs of Shaker Heights and Cleveland Heights in Cleveland, Ohio. Her father, Albert Struven, worked as a civil engineer and vice president of a construction company that built oil refineries and steel plants around the world, earning a nice income that provided his family with the finer things in life. Jean attended the Cleveland area's leading private school, the Laurel School, before heading to Smith College, a prestigious, private liberal arts college for women in Northampton, Massachusetts. Former classmates claimed she was ambitious and personable. She was elected to Phi Beta Kappa and graduated magna cum laude with an economics degree in 1945.

Soon after receiving her diploma from Smith, Jean married James Harris, the son of a mid-level chemicals executive from Detroit. They began their new life together in a two-story colonial house on a tree-lined street in Grosse Pointe, Michigan. James took a job as a supervisor at the Holly Carburetor Company. In 1946, four months after exchanging wedding vows with James, Jean obtained a position teaching history and current events at the private Grosse Pointe Country Day School.

She remained at home for several years to start a family. The first Harris son, David, was born in 1950. Soon after a second son, James, arrived in 1952, Jean returned to the school to work as a first-grade teacher. While living in Grosse Pointe, Jean earned a master's degree in education from Wayne State University in Detroit.

But her picturesque life started to crumble in 1964. First, she was passed over for a promotion at work. Then, in October, she filed for divorce on the grounds of extreme and repeated cruelty. Jean asked for custody of the two boys and possession of the house on the condition that James continue to pay the mortgage. The divorce was granted on February 23, 1965, dissolving the nineteen-year marriage.

The following year Jean decided she needed a change of scenery, and she secured a position as the director of the middle school at the Springside School for girls in Philadelphia, Pennsylvania. She and her sons moved from Grosse Pointe in September 1966, and found a house in Chestnut Hill, one of Philadelphia's finer neighborhoods.

A friend from childhood, Marge Richey Jacobson, and her husband, Leslie, soon introduced Jean to a cardiologist, Dr. Herman Tarnower, who was thirteen years older than Jean. A confirmed bachelor, the physician was often seen at social events in the company of attractive women.

Herman Tarnower's Jewish family was solidly middle class. His father owned a prosperous New York business that manufactured hats. Herman, known as "Hy" to his friends, studied medicine at Syracuse and graduated in 1933. After completing a residency at Bellevue, he obtained a postgraduate fellowship in cardiology with six months of study in London and six months in Amsterdam.

By 1939 Hy was an attending cardiologist at White Plains Hospital. During World War II he served in the US Army Medical Corps and was stationed in Japan. Returning home from the war, he established a cardiology practice known as the Scarsdale Medical Group, in partnership with Dr. John Cannon, in the Scarsdale and White Plains areas of New York.

From their first meeting in 1966, Jean and Hy were mutually attracted to each other. Over the next few years, their relationship grew and deepened. Jean was linked, arm in arm, with Hy at dinner parties and New York events with high-profile guests. In 1972 Jean strategically arranged to be closer to the physician's home in Purchase, New York. She left her position in Philadelphia to become the headmistress of the Thomas School, a private girls' school in Rowayton, Connecticut, and she purchased a home in Mahopac, New York—a forty-five minute drive between the school and Hy's house.

After the Thomas School merged with another educational institution in 1975, Jean left private education to assume a position with the Allied Maintenance Corporation as a sales supervisor. Within eighteen months, however, she learned about an opening for a headmistress at the Madeira School in McLean, Virginia, on the outskirts of the nation's capital.

The Madeira School, founded in 1906, was the crown jewel in private education for girls. With a 100 percent college acceptance rate, Madeira attracted the daughters of politicians and celebrities to its campus, which had just been equipped with an indoor equestrian riding ring. When the current headmistress retired in 1977, the board of alumnae reviewed one hundred applications to fill the position. Jean Struven Harris seemed to be the perfect candidate—a refined woman with management skills along with knowledge and experience in private education.

Later that year Jean was appointed headmistress of Madeira. She frequently traveled to Purchase, New York, for weekends with Hy, but the physician seemed to become more distant with each passing month. By early 1978 he was also becoming more preoccupied with a popular diet that he had developed for his heart patients. For years Hy had given the diet information to his patients on a single mimeographed page. After the *New York Times* featured the diet, author Samm Sinclair Baker and Hy discussed the idea of jointly writing a book on the topic. They decided to use the question-and-answer format for readers.

Writing night and day for more than four months, they completed the manuscript on October 1, 1978. When *The Complete Scarsdale Medical Diet* was released in 1979, it was an immediate bestseller. The book sold 750,000 hardback copies and another two million paperback copies. Every edition featured a prominent acknowledgment to Jean Harris.

Along with his new fame and fortune as a popular author, Dr. Herman Tarnower was making another change in his life. Lynne Tryforos, an attractive, blonde medical assistant at the Scarsdale Medical Group, was frequently seen in the company of the physician. They went to dinner parties and New York functions together—the same type of events that Hy and Jean had attended as a couple for nearly fourteen years.

Hy's affair hit Jean with full force. The new woman in the doctor's life was twenty years younger than Jean, a fact that seemed especially cruel to an aging woman in her late fifties. Though she attempted to hide her grief and depression, the girls at Madeira noticed dramatic changes in her personality and behavior. They would later contend that she seemed extremely nervous during this period, always tugging at her hair, walking with a slump, and never in a jovial mood. At one point a girl asked a harmless question during an assembly, and Jean burst into tears while standing on the stage in front of the entire school.

In December 1979 Hy took Jean to Palm Beach to spend Christmas and the New Year with friends. They spent their time relaxing, reading, and talking, and Jean probably thought their relationship was improving. But within thirty days Hy was taking another trip, traveling to Montego Bay, Jamaica, with another woman at his side: Lynne Tryforos.

By early March Jean Harris had reached the depths of despair. Over the weekend of March 8 and 9, she remained secluded in her home, contemplating a future without Dr. Herman Tarnower. On Monday, March 10, 1980, she wrote a long, rambling letter to the physician and took it to the post office on the Madeira campus. She sent the letter by registered mail, which required a signature from the recipient upon delivery.

Late in the day Jean dressed in a black dress suit with a white shirt for a sit-down dinner for fourteen at the home of some friends later that evening. Before leaving, she scribbled some notes about her intentions, writing that she never intended to return home, and scattered the notes around the house.

Jean apparently decided not to attend the dinner party. She located her gun, a .32-caliber revolver that she had purchased some years ago, and tossed the weapon, still in the original box, into her car. Then she headed north in the direction of the home of Dr. Herman Tarnower in Purchase, New York.

Jean would later reveal that she intended to visit Hy one last time and then shoot herself near a patch of daffodils that always bloomed in the spring by the pond on his estate. She had plenty of time to think about the ideal spot for pulling the trigger during the five-hour drive from the Virginia suburbs of Washington to New York's Westchester County. A thunderstorm erupted during the trip, and sheets of rain blanketed the Tarnower estate when she arrived.

She stormed into Hy's bedroom, her gun hidden in a pocket. He was in the bed, sleeping alone, clad in beige pajamas. Jean suddenly noticed some unwelcome sights in the room—a negligee, jewelry, and hair curlers that she could only assume belonged to Lynn Tryforos. Jean would later testify that she slipped the gun out of her pocket and announced her intent to kill herself. Hy tried to wrestle the gun from her hands. During the struggle the gun went off, mortally wounding the physician.

A burglary call came into the local police station at one minute before eleven o'clock. A patrolman arrived within minutes to find the body of Herman Tarnower, eight days before his seventieth birthday, sprawled awkwardly on the bed. As the victim uttered a few unintelligible words, Jean Harris stood silently nearby, distraught, rain-drenched, and in apparent shock.

Outside the house Jean rambled, contradicting herself. At one point she admitted she shot and killed Herman Tarnower. But she also insisted she had asked him to kill her.

With no other witnesses or suspects at hand, police arrested Jean Struven Harris on the spot and booked her on charges of second-degree murder. Jean made a phone call to her friends, Marge and Leslie Jacobson, who had introduced her to Herman Tarnower. Leslie quickly arranged for an attorney to represent Jean.

When the news broke, the media and the public were instantly captivated by the story of the elegant, sophisticated, educated woman who had been scorned by the celebrity diet doctor and tossed aside for a much younger woman. When she arrived at the doctor's home on that rainy March night, was she intent on killing herself—or him? As the public awaited the murder trial, that question was debated in newspapers and magazines, on television and radio talk shows, and at cocktail parties and water coolers, for nearly a year.

More than one hundred reporters arrived in Westchester County for the trial in early 1981. Jean testified for eight days on the witness stand, charming onlookers with her quiet, dignified elegance and sharp wit. At one point she recalled a birthday message from Lynn Tryforos to the physician that appeared in a small advertisement on the front page of the *New York Times*. Jean couldn't help but mention the ad to Hy. "Herman, why don't you use the Goodyear blimp next time? I think it's available," she recalled saying.

After eight days of deliberation, the jury found her guilty of second-degree murder on February 28, 1981. Though Jean had claimed the shooting was accidental, jurors found her version of the story contradicted the evidence. She could not account for the multiple bullet wounds in Hy's body, including one in his back and another in the palm of his hand, that indicated he was trying to defend himself from an attack.

Jean Struven Harris initially had a difficult adjustment to life at New York's Bedford Hills Correctional Facility for Women, horrified by the number of incarcerated women housed at the maximum security prison who had followed in their own mothers' footsteps to live behind locked prison doors. Within a few years she established herself as an authority on the special problems faced by children of imprisoned mothers. Determined to break the cycle of second-generation female prisoners, she lobbied to create a prison nursery to house the children of inmates. Her efforts succeeded, and the first prison nursery in the United States soon opened under the name of the Children's Center at Bedford Hills.

With her model behavior, Jean was moved from a regular cell block to the prison's Fiske Building, a less confining residence with private rooms for inmates who had proven themselves to be trustworthy. Jean filled the long days of confinement by constantly reading and putting pen to paper. While incarcerated, Jean wrote three books: *Marking Time, Stranger in Two Worlds*, and *They Always Call Us Ladies*, chronicling her ordeal, her life before and during prison, and her new work on behalf of imprisoned mothers and their children.

Since she was considered to be a model prisoner, her attorney asked New York governor Mario Cuomo for clemency in her case. Clemency would allow the possibility of an early parole before the end of her fifteen-year sentence. But the governor, a potential Democratic presidential candidate, rejected the plea three times, maintaining that Jean Harris was no different than any other scorned woman who had killed her ex-lover. Still, thousands of people across the United States supported her early release from prison. One of her sons even collected signatures in support of early release from a table set up on a street corner in Manhattan.

But the three devastating rejections for clemency and the constant stress of confinement took their toll on Jean Harris. Even though heart disease did not run in her family, she suffered three heart attacks during her prison stay. Her doctors claimed the "distress of confinement" had provoked the attacks. "I honestly thought I would die in prison," Jean later recalled.

She vowed she would refuse treatment in the event of a fourth heart attack, primarily because she despised being transported in manacles, which were mandated for prisoner transport.

But a fourth heart attack required bypass surgery, and Jean was in no shape to argue about treatment. On December 29, 1992, just as Jean was being prepared for the bypass procedure, she was stunned to receive a message from the governor's office. Governor Mario Cuomo had granted her fourth request for clemency. "I woke up at three a.m. and made the decision at four a.m.," he told the Associated Press. Cuomo admitted he had agonized over the decision to commute her sentence, but her failing health had convinced him to grant the clemency request.

Still weeping with joy, Jean was wheeled into the operating room a few hours after learning the news. Following several months of recovery, she was released from prison after serving twelve years of her fifteen-year sentence. By April 1993 she had moved to a small cabin on the Connecticut River, becoming an official resident of New Hampshire—the state with the motto of "Live Free or Die."

At the time of her release, Jean Struven Harris was nearly seventy years old. She spent her remaining years avoiding the limelight, writing an occasional article, tending to her garden, and enjoying walks with her golden retriever.

But the life of Jean Struven Harris remained a subject of public fascination long after her release from prison. Actress Annette Bening played the title role of the former school headmistress in the 2006 television movie *Mrs. Harris*. The film was the second movie portraying the ordeals of the Ohio native. Shortly after the trial ended in 1981, actress Ellen Burstyn starred in the television movie, *The People vs. Jean Harris*.

Jean Harris died from natural causes on Sunday, December 23, 2012, at an assisted living facility in New Haven, Connecticut. She was eighty-nine years old.

Bibliography

Dr. John Cook Bennett

Flake, Lawrence R. *Prophets and Apostles of the Last Dispensation.* Provo, UT: Religious Studies Center, Brigham Young University, 2001.

Smith, Andrew F. "'The Diploma Pedler': Dr. John Cook Bennett and the Christian College, New Albany, Indiana," *Indiana Magazine of History*, Vol. 90, Issue 1, March 1994.

———. *The Saintly Scoundrel: The Life and Times of Dr. John Cook Bennett.* Urbana and Chicago, IL: University of Illinois Press, 1997.

Waite, Frederick C. "The First Medical Diploma Mill in the United States," *Bulletin of the History of Medicine*, January 1, 1946.

John Chivington

Cox-Paul, Lori. "John M. Chivington: The 'Reverend Colonel' 'Marry-Your-Daughter' 'Sand Creek Massacre,'" *Nebraska History*, Winter 2007.

Craig, Reginald S. *The Fighting Parson: The Biography of Colonel John M. Chivington.* Los Angeles, CA: Westernlore Press, 1959.

George H. Devol

Devol, George H. *Forty Years a Gambler on the Mississippi.* Cincinnati, OH: Devol & Haines, 1887.

Mayo, Matthew P. *Hornswogglers, Fourflushers & Snake-Oil Salesmen: True Tales of the Old West.* Guilford, CT: Rowman & Littlefield, 2015.

McManus, James. *Cowboys Full: The Story of Poker.* New York, NY: Farrar, Straus, and Giroux, 2009.

Patterson, Benton Rain. *The Great American Steamboat Race: The Natchez and the Robert E. Lee and the Climax of an Era*. Jefferson, NC: McFarland & Company, Inc., 2009.

Nancy Farrer

Cooley, Thomas. *The Ivory Leg in the Ebony Cabinet: Madness, Race, and Gender in Victorian America*. Amherst, MA: University of Massachusetts Press, 2001.

Howells, William D. *Sketch of the Life and Character of Rutherford B. Hayes*. Boston, MA: Hurd and Houghton, 1876.

Quinn, J. J., M.D. "Homicidal Insanity—The Case of Nancy Farrer," *Western Lancet: A Monthly Journal of Practical Medicine and Surgery*, Vol. 16, No. 11, November 1855.

Victoria Claflin Woodhull

Gabriel, Mary. *Notorious Victoria: The Life of Victoria Woodhull, Uncensored*. Chapel Hill, NC: Algonquin Books, 1998.

Havelin, Kate. *Victoria Woodhull: Fearless Feminist*. Minneapolis, MN: Twenty-first Century Books, 2007.

Pirok, Alena R. "Mrs. Satan's Penance: The New History of Victoria Woodhull," *Legacy*, Vol. 11, No. 1, Article 4, 2011.

Stephen Wallace Dorsey

Bailey, Thomas Anderson. *Presidential Saints and Sinners*. New York, NY: The Free Press, 1981.

Caffey, David L. *Chasing the Santa Fe Ring: Power and Privilege in Territorial New Mexico*. Albuquerque, NM: University of New Mexico Press, 2014.

Grana, Mari. *On the Fringes of Power: The Life and Turbulent Career of Stephen Wallace Dorsey*. Guilford, CT: TwoDot Books, 2015.

Wilkerson, Lyn R. *American Trails Revisited: Following in the Footsteps of the Western Pioneers*. Lincoln, NE: iUniverse, 2003.

Cassie Chadwick

Abbott, Karen. "The High Priestess of Fraudulent Finance," *Smithsonian Magazine*, June 27, 2012.

Butts, Ed. *She Dared: True Stories of Heroines, Scoundrels, and Renegades*. New York, NY: Random House, 2009.

Segrave, Kerry. *Women Swindlers in America, 1860-1920*. Jefferson, NC: McFarland & Company, Inc., Publishers, 2007.

Alfred Knapp

Jones, Richard O. *The First Celebrity Serial Killer in Southwest Ohio: Confessions of the Strangler Alfred Knapp*. Charleston, SC: The History Press, 2015.

Kennedy, Rick. "The Devil She Knew," *Cincinnati Magazine*, November 10, 2014.

"Knapp Will Die for All His Crimes," *The Cincinnati Times-Star*, June 29, 1904.

Dr. James Howard Snook

Franklin, Diana Britt, with Nancy Pennell. *Gold Medal Killer*. Spokane, WA: Marquette Books, LLC, 2010.

Gribben, Mark. *The Professor and the Co-ed*. Charleston, SC: The History Press, 2010.

Meyers, David, and Elise Meyers Walker. *Historic Columbus Crimes*. Charleston, SC: The History Press, 2010.

Phillips, Otto W. "The Mystery of the Thirteenth Key," *True Detective Mysteries*, January 1930.

Eva Brickel Kaber

Bellamy II, John Stark. *They Died Crawling and Other Tales of Cleveland Woe*. Cleveland, OH: Gray & Company, Publishers, 2005.

"Mrs. Kaber Escapes Death Penalty," *The Pittsburg Press*, July 17, 1921, page 3.

Simmons, Ariel W. "Pinkerton's National Detective Agency, Part B: Criminal Case File, Series 3 'K'–'N'," *Research Collections in American Legal History*, Bethesda, MD: Lexis Nexis, 2009.

Martha Wise

Bellamy II, John Stark. *Women Behaving Badly: True Tales of Cleveland's Most Ferocious Female Killers*. Cleveland, OH: Gray & Company, Publishers, 2005.

Bovsun, Mara. "The Poison Widow of Hardscrabble," *New York Daily News*, March 25, 2008.

"Had 'Funeral Complex'—Mrs. Martha Wise Poisoned Seventeen Persons and Set Fire to Houses and Barns," *Evening State Journal* (Lincoln, NE), March 20, 1925.

Nelson, Ben. "The Devil in Hardscrabble Alley," *The American Weekly* (San Antonio, TX), January 4, 1942.

"Poison Widow Back in Cell," *The Daily Reporter* (Dover, OH), February 2, 1962.

Charles Arthur "Pretty Boy" Floyd

Brookes, Timothy. "The Death of Pretty Boy Floyd," East Liverpool Historical Society, 1994, www.eastliverpoolhistoricalsociety.org/pbfloyd1.htm, accessed February 1, 2016.

King, Jeffery S. *The Life and Death of Pretty Boy Floyd*. Kent, OH: The Kent State University Press, 1998.

Wallis, Michael. *Pretty Boy: The Life and Times of Charles Arthur Floyd*. New York, NY: W. W. Norton & Co., Inc., 1992.

Anna Marie Hahn

Franklin, Diana Britt. "A Poison Mind," *Cincinnati Magazine*, October 2006.

Lauter, Evelyn. "The Blonde Borgia," *Cincinnati Magazine*, December 1989.

Shipman, Marlin. *The Penalty is Death: US Newspaper Coverage of Women's Executions*. Columbia, MO: University of Missouri Press, 2002.

Streib, Victor L. *The Fairer Death: Executing Women in Ohio*. Athens, OH: Ohio University Press, 2006.

Edythe Klumpp

Conrad, Barry. "Edythe Klumpp Rare Interview," Barcon Productions, 1959.

Jones, Richard O. *Cincinnati's Savage Seamstress: The Shocking Edythe Klumpp Murder Scandal*. Charleston, SC: The History Press, 2014.

Schulz, Janice. *Cincinnati's Celebrity Criminal Defender: Murder, Motive & the Magical Foss Hopkins*. Charleston SC: The History Press, 2015.

Souder, Dan. "Murder Revisited," *Cincinnati Magazine*, Vol. 29, No. 11, August 1996.

Uhlenbrock, Doug. "1959: State of Ohio v. Edythe Margaret Klumpp," *Cincinnati Magazine*, August 2001.

Jean Struven Harris

Alexander, Shana. "The Case for Jean Harris," *New York Magazine*, April 7, 1986.

Berger, Joseph. "Headmistress, Jilted Lover, Killer, Then a Force for Good in Jail," *New York Times*, December 28, 2012.

Haden-Guest, Anthony. "The Headmistress and the Diet Doctor," *New York Magazine*, March 31, 1980.

Kilian, Michael. "Jean Harris: Her Life Behind Bars," *Chicago Tribune*, August 3, 1986.

Warrick, Pamela. "'The Myth of Me': Aftermath," *Los Angeles Times*, July 19, 1993.

Index

Chadwick, Leroy S., 65–66, 68
Cheyenne tribe, 16
Chivington, Isaac, 12, 13
Chivington, Isabella Amzen, 20
Chivington, Jane Runyon, 12,
    13, 19, 20
Chivington, John, 12–22
  childhood, 12, 13
  death, 22
  divorce, 19
  family, 12, 13, 17–18
  government, claims against,
    21–22
  legal troubles, 18–19, 20, 21
  marriages, 13, 17–18, 20
  military career, 14, 16, 17,
    20–21, 22
  ministerial career, 12, 13–14
  photo, 15
  political career, 17, 20
  slavery, stance against,
    12, 14
Chivington, Lewis, 12, 13
Chivington, Lulu, 17
Chivington, Martha Rollason,
    13, 17
Chivington, Sarah, 17–18, 19
Chivington, Thomas, 17, 18
Christian church, 3–4, 6, 9–10
Christian College, 4–8, 9, 10
Citizen's National Bank, 67,
    68, 69
Claflin, Anna, 41, 42
Claflin, Buck, 41–42, 44, 45
Claflin, Tennessee "Tennie," 42,

43–44, 45, 47, 48–49
Classical, Literary, and Sci-
    entific Institution of the
    Scioto Valley, 8–9
Colavito, Erminia, 98–99, 101
*Complete Scarsdale Medical
    Diet, The* (Tarnower and
    Baker), 147
con artists. *See* Chadwick,
    Cassie; Dorsey, Stephen
    Wallace
Conkle, Ellen, 112, 114, 121
Corrigan, William J., 99–100
Cuomo, Mario, 150–51

D
Davey, Martin, 131
Devere, Lydia. *See* Chadwick,
    Cassie
Devol, George H., 23–31
  charitable actions, 30–31
  childhood, 25
  disguises, 27–28
  escapes, 27
  gambling, 23–25, 26,
    28–30, 31
  imprisonment, 28
  ministers and, 28–30
  physical prowess, 26–27
  portrait, 24
  soldiers and, 28
Devol, Paul, 25, 26
Dillinger, John, 120
Dillon, Bertha, 83–84
Dillon, James, 60, 62, 66

fortune-tellers. *See*
spiritualism
*Forty Years a Gambler on the
Mississippi* (Devol), 24,
30, 31
free love, 39, 46, 47, 48
Frinkle, David, 95
Fultz, J. H., 120

G
gambling, 23–25, 26, 28–30, 31
Gard, Warren, 75, 77
Gardner, Virginia, 129
Garfield, James G., 55–57
Gebhart, Ada, 73, 76
Gienke, Fred, 105, 106, 107
Gienke, Lillian, 105, 106, 107,
108, 109–10
Gienke, Marie, 106–7
Gienke, Richard, 107–8
Gienke, Rudolph, 106–7
Granville Baptist College, 9
Green, Mrs., 35
Gsellman, George, 126, 127
Gusweiler, Frank M., 133,
138–39, 140
Guthrie, Woody, 121

H
Hahn, Anna Marie, 122–31
appearance/dress, 129
childhood, 122, 124
death, 131
marriage, 124
photo, 123

poison victims, 125, 126,
127–30
son, 124, 126, 127, 130, 131
trial, 127–31
Hahn, Philip, 124, 125, 127
Hamilton County Lunatic
Asylum, 37–38
Harris, James, 145
Harris, Jean Struven, 143–52
childhood, 144–45
children, 145
clemency requests, 150–51
divorce, 145
as educator, 145, 146,
147–48
health, 151
imprisonment, 143–44,
150–51
marriage, 145
movies about, 152
photo, 144
trial, 143, 149–50
Hasel, Fred, 105
Hasel, Martha. *See* Wise,
Martha
Hasel, Sophie Gienke, 102, 105,
106, 107, 108
Hayes, Rutherford B., 33, 34,
36, 37
Heis, George, 125, 128–29
Hilderbrand, Fred, 117
Hildreth, Samuel P., 2
Hix, Melvin T., 83
Hix, Theora Kathleen, 80,
82–84, 86, 87, 88, 89–90

About the Author

Susan Sawyer enjoys exploring the past and writing about historical topics. History serves as the centerpiece for much of her writing, taking form in both fact and fiction. Susan is the author of seventeen books, including *Ohio's Remarkable Women*, 2nd edition, *More Than Petticoats: Remarkable Tennessee Women*, *It Happened in Tennessee*, and *Myths and Mysteries of Tennessee* (all by Globe Pequot Press).

A graduate of the University of Tennessee, Susan worked as a magazine editor and communications consultant before establishing a career as a freelance writer and published author. Today she writes from her home in the suburbs of Chattanooga, Tennessee.